Good Morning, Beautiful

ALWAYS PRIORITIZED BY THE MAN

WHO IS THE STANDARD OF LOVE

MAKEYA KINARD

Rights Department, 2442 Michelle Drive, Tustin, CA 92780.
Trilogy Christian Publishing/ TBN and colophon are trademarks of
Trinity Broadcasting Network.

For information about special discounts for bulk purchases, please
contact Trilogy Christian Publishing.

Trilogy Disclaimer: The views and content expressed in this book
are those of the author and may not necessarily reflect the views and
doctrine of Trilogy Christian Publishing or the Trinity Broadcasting
Network.

10 9 8 7 6 5 4 3 2 1
Library of Congress Cataloging-in-Publication Data is available.
ISBN 979-9-89041-993-4
ISBN (ebook) 979-9-89041-994-1

Dedication

To the one searching for a place to belong--

"For I know the plans I have for you, says the Lord. They are plans for good and not for disaster, to give you a future and a hope. In those days when you pray, I will listen. If you look for me wholeheartedly, you will find me. I will be found by you, says the Lord. I will end your captivity and restore your fortunes. I will gather you out of the nations where I sent you and will bring you home again to your own land."

Jeremiah 29:11-14 NLT

Acknowledgments

I want to take this opportunity to express my gratitude to my family, whose unwavering support and encouragement have been a constant source of inspiration throughout my journey. To my mom and dad, thank you for teaching me the importance of faith and obedience to God. You have instilled in me the significance of making the right choices, even in difficult situations, and the value of prioritizing my relationship with God. To my siblings, your constant presence and reassurance have given me the courage to step out of my comfort zone and open my heart to others. To my grandparents, thank you for sharing your wisdom and encouraging me to stay on the path. I am grateful to you all for your trust in God's plan for my life.

I would like to express my sincere gratitude to my circle of friends who have been there every step of the way. You have shown me the importance of sharing my feelings and the true value of giving and receiving. I am grateful for your wisdom, attentive listening, and words of encouragement, which have inspired me to share my story. Words cannot adequately convey how much I appreciate each and every one of you.

Introduction

Listen here, friend: singleness is a season, not your identity, and if there is one thing that stands true about seasons, it is that they change. However, with each season, there is a process that allows you to grow and evolve into the next phase of your life. Praying, fasting, and waiting are part of the journey, but your obedience to God is equally important.

To grow into something new, we need to let go of what's holding us back. Change can be unfamiliar, but it's necessary to reach our full potential. This season is about more than just finding a spouse; it's about discovering who we are meant to be in the eyes of God.

So here you are, and I am happy you are choosing to stay in the race! Waiting is hard; unfortunately, there are no shortcuts when you decide to do things God's way. It is okay if you find this process uncomfortable, or maybe you dread committing fully because you are unsure if things will work out in your favor. But guess what? We weren't created to know but rather have faith and trust in God.

The Bible is a web of knowledge, and though the stories and parables are of people who have come and gone, their legacy still lives to this day. We can see the God of Abraham, Isaac, and Jacob coming to life in many people's stories and testimonies. God wants to be present in yours as well.

Good Morning, Beautiful is a six week devotional designed to help singles and anyone looking to enhance their walk with God. In each devotional, we explore scriptures to help you uncover God's message.

This book is a collection of personal stories that detail my journey. Drawing insights from God's Word, I explore the implications of its teachings on real-life situations, offering valuable revelations along the way. I know how it feels to wish for a friend who can understand your struggles, and I want to offer that same support to you as you work towards overcoming your challenges. I believe that sharing stories is the best way to bring Scripture to life through personal experiences. Also, at the end of each devotional is a daily challenge to help you learn how to apply His word to your current circumstances. This is your season of learning and entering a new phase of transformation as you continue in your walk with God.

I am excited about what God has planned. My prayer for you is that through these devotionals, you will feel encouraged to step outside of your box and society's standards for what this season must look like and instead walk in the purpose God has called you to. Each day, God wants to greet you and make each encounter personal. Your relationship with Christ will allow you to better understand His standards. In return, you will have a greater desire to strive for nothing less than what our Heavenly Father desires for you.

Sincerely,

Your Friend

TABLE OF CONTENTS

Week 1

The Girl Behind Her Smile

If anyone truly knows me, you will see that I smile at every little thing. Sometimes, it aggravates my sisters so much, but guess what? It's who I am. However, my smile has changed over the years in a good way, but before I became who I am today, my smile was a façade hiding the emptiness I didn't want others to see. I still remember when mountains of heartache and pain lay behind that smile. I have pictures to prove it! As I look through Facebook and Instagram, which house all my photos from grade school to the first parts of college, I can vividly see the pain I once felt. I can see the force behind my smile to appear happy.

Truthfully, I was angry, jealous, hateful, self-conscious, and lonely. Much of my pain resulted from the many insecurities I carried as a child. I remember the days of looking in the mirror and hating my reflection. I was so distraught with my appearance that my lack of confidence began to show, and others saw it. One day, my mom saw me upset and irritable. She attempted to help me dismantle the lies I believed about myself. She told me to just look in the mirror and find something I loved. With all my strength, I tried my hardest to see beauty in my face, skin, and size, but I just couldn't.

In my attempts to avoid these discussions, I hid by being the girl behind the scenes, not wanting to be in the spotlight, and not wanting to be known even though deep down I wanted attention. I wanted someone to recognize me but couldn't even recognize myself. My mom attempted to input wisdom as she warned me about what feeling insecure could do. She told me that even in my attempts to hide, other people could see that. I wish I had listened, because I found myself in unhealthy relationships, chasing after people who did not deserve my time. I also found myself broken after hearing the words others would say about me. I often say, "I wish I knew then what I know now." Now, I'm in a better state of mind and can see myself through a better lens. I understand what my mom was trying to warn me about. Our insecurities carry a scent; they may not be noticeable to us, but they are inviting for all the wrong reasons.

Maybe today, you've struggled with who you are and do not understand how you find yourself around unhealthy people. Perhaps you are struggling with the pain behind your smile, but I want to tell you that you aren't alone. You will soon experience what it means to have a genuine smile that will brighten any room you enter, but first, we must take apart the areas of our lives rooted in our pain. We must come face to face with the girl in the mirror.

This week is all about starting the journey toward change. God wants you to see your reflection and come face to face with your giants. He wants to take you to a place of true fulfillment and pleasure. So hold on, and let's get into it because God has a message for you!

Week 1

Day 1

Something Needs to Change

Good morning, beautiful.

I vividly remember a saying my mom would tell me when she saw me lacking or struggling to have a backbone. She would say, "When you get sick and tired of being sick and tired, you'll do something." It wasn't until I became an adult that I understood what my mom had been trying to tell me. She taught me that when you reach your breaking point, you will stop allowing things to "just happen." You will find your voice and do something about it!

Stepping outside of your comfort zone is never easy, especially when you reach a point in your life where you realize that you can't keep doing the same thing and hoping for different results. Change is never comfortable, but it is necessary. Just like you need basic necessities such as food, water, and clothes to live, you need "change" to evolve into the person you were destined to become.

The first step to change is realizing that you must get off the hamster wheel and stop avoiding areas in your life that must be addressed. The second step is knowing who to turn to. So today,

I invite you to take the chance and try God. That yearning in your heart is there for a reason; don't be afraid to move forward. Understand your journey may look a little different, but trust and believe it serves the same purpose: to fulfill God's will here on this earth (read Hebrews 10:36).

Sincerely,

Your friend

A Moment to Reflect

*"Now the LORD had said unto Abram, Get thee out of thy country,
and from thy kindred, and from thy father's house,
unto a land that I will shew thee."*

Genesis 12:1

Can you imagine being told to leave your home and family? I
don't know about you, but I would feel all out of place and anxious.
However, God said this very thing to Abraham, and he obeyed.
He needed to leave his home and begin a journey that led him into
unfamiliarity but true fulfillment. As God said, "Get *thee out of thy
country, and from thy kindred, and from thy father's house"* (v. 1), God
was telling Abraham that he must separate from the things of his past.

To advance in God's kingdom, we must rid ourselves of the old.
God must pull you out of something to take you somewhere because
you can't inherit the promises of God by staying where you are. You
must be transformed by the spirit of God, meaning that we can no
longer see life through the lenses of our flesh but rather by the Holy
Spirit (see Romans 12:2).

Transformation is a "dramatic change in form or appearance,"
according to the Oxford Dictionary. A prime example is, of course,
Abraham. If you haven't noticed, when his name changed it made
his transformation known. Abraham was once called Abram. I want
you to pay special attention to the fact that the name change didn't
happen immediately (see Genesis 12-17:5). Abram experienced a
series of tests and trials. Still, when God gave him the vision and
established his purpose, his name represented his new identity
in Christ. He was no longer called Abram "exalted father" but
Abraham, meaning "father of many nations" (see Genesis 17:5).

In your season of waiting, God may be calling you to separate from things, not to hurt you but because He sees the fullness of who you are and what you can be. So much so that your blessing is attached to your new name, but you must be open to waiting and allowing God to prepare you for your promise. The beauty of Abraham is that he didn't fully know what God had in store for him, but when God called him out, he said yes, and because of his yes, he became a changed man with a changed name and a changed future. Does this remind you of someone? I hope you're pointing at yourself!

When we are obedient to God, we tell Him that His ways are higher than ours and that we trust Him with our lives. To submit to God and His calling, we allow our obedience to be a sacrifice. Abraham's sacrifices on his journey consisted of surrendering his native land, family, the Vale of Jordan, riches of Sodom, self, Ishmael (the son Hagar bore him), and Isaac (the promise).[1] It sounds like a lot, and I am sure it took much strength for Abraham to obey. However, each surrender opened the door for growth because of his obedience. God is leading you in the way of increase, but first you must separate and make sacrifices.

Sometimes, it takes reaching our breaking point to look up and realize that our lives are nowhere near the life God created for us. God is here to restore your hope and open your eyes to the future He has for you. Just as God called Abraham out of his home, God called you out of your current position. He is inviting you on a journey to travel to the land He has destined for you. Understand that God is strategic in His planning, and what seemed like the end is actually your beginning.

DAILY CHALLENGE

Spend time to meditate on today's message and list areas in your life that are problematic or of great concern to you. Take your list before God and ask Him where to start.

Day 2

The Power of One Action

Good morning, beautiful.

To mature as Christians, we must learn to hold on to the Word of God, because it says, "Now the ones that fell among thorns are those who, when they have heard, go out and are choked with cares, riches, and pleasures of life, and bring no fruit to maturity" (see Luke 8:14 NKJV). Reading God's Word or attending a service and hearing a powerful message can feel exciting and liberating. Still, we must be aware that many things in this world are designed to choke the seeds that God has planted and stump our ability to grow.

Like a seed that must undergo a process to reach its full potential, Christians must shift their perspective on life to develop and grow. True growth requires accountability for our actions, resisting the urge to blame others, an open-minded approach to criticism (not being so defensive), and doing the right thing even when it's difficult. Without growth, God's blessings cannot be fully realized. We must be ready to receive and properly handle the precious gifts that God has assigned to us by committing to personal development. In other words, change begins with you!

Today is another opportunity to expand your horizons and evolve. I pray that God opens your heart to desire more of Him and that you use this moment to strengthen your faith and increase self-awareness. Lord, I ask that You reveal Your purpose and true intentions to the reader and take us on a journey to experience You. In Jesus's name, Amen!

Sincerely,

Your friend

A Moment to Reflect

"When I was a child, I spake as a child, I understood as a child, I thought as a child: but when I became a man, I put away childish things."

1 Corinthians 13:11

You think that as you age, things will become easier. As children, we assume that everything will come together in adulthood. Unfortunately, that is not the case. It takes experience, patience, and perseverance to manage life. Wisdom and knowledge are gifts we obtain when we learn from our mistakes and overcome challenges. There are a lot of growing pains when aging, and to be mature, we must evolve from our carnal states, "the flesh," and become more spiritually sound so we can interpret the Holy Spirit and God's will for our lives (see 1 Corinthians 3:1-3).

To mature in Christ, we must *"Put away childish things"* (v. 11). So, what does that mean? It means leaving behind the "Me first" attitude. If you haven't been around children lately, I can tell you that they can be a little selfish sometimes, like when they tell us, "No, I don't want to do that, or that's mine; I don't want to share." Sadly, some of us still carry this same thought process into adulthood. The first step to putting away childish things is to develop better self-awareness. Self-awareness allows us to reassess our actions and behaviors and rid ourselves of what is causing havoc. For example, when we sense that someone has done us wrong, we will have an open heart and use effective communication skills instead of wanting to fight or speak ill towards that person. Also, instead of cutting people from our lives, we will understand and begin to set healthy boundaries.

In this journey, you will realize that maturity is necessary to survive. As we mature, we learn to let go of our selfish desires and put the needs of others before our own. We begin to see the world through a lens of compassion and empathy, recognizing the inherent dignity of every human being. This allows us to love others as Christ has loved us. Maturity also helps us navigate life's difficulties with grace and resilience. When we encounter challenges and setbacks, we can draw on our faith and trust in God's plan for our lives. We know that even in the midst of suffering, God is working for our good and will never abandon us. Only God can shape our worldview and put everything in the proper perspective (see 1 Corinthians 14:33).

Everything that God has produced serves a greater purpose in its mature state. No one can remain a child forever, because that is not how God designed humanity. His intent was for us to grow, and if you look at all aspects of life (babies, plants, animals), no one thing remains small and feeble. Therefore, God wants you in a place of freedom, meaning without constraints. The weights that hold us down are nothing more than mental chains we can break with one thought. The power of one action can create a domino effect of change. As we evolve, we elevate from core beliefs, such as "I am unlovable, worthless, or helpless," to "I am safe, my needs are met, and I can forgive."

I encourage you to embrace your identity in Christ and trust the ongoing journey of development and transformation. As you strive to deepen your relationship with God, His love and grace will continuously shape and refine you, with the comfort of knowing He is always by your side.

Daily Challenge

In every choice we make, there is a consequence, whether positive or negative. Reflect on a recent choice you made that has changed your life. Now I want you to answer the following questions:

1. Did you pray about it before deciding?
2. Did you have patience waiting on God to answer?
3. When you made the choice, were you thinking from a carnal state, or did you allow the Holy Spirit to guide you?

I want to stress that life is all about trying again. Don't feel defeated if a past choice did not pan out as you intended. God is in the midst of it all, but He is waiting for you to look to Him so He can guide you on what to do next!

Day 3

Don't Imagine the Wrong Attack

Good morning, beautiful.

Don't you just love catching up with a friend and chatting for hours on end? I always leave these conversations with new insights that help me grow in my faith. Recently, a conversation with a friend taught me an important lesson – not to anticipate the wrong attacks. My friend advised me to remain prayerful so I could better identify where the enemy's attacks were coming from. I am grateful for her guidance because it's easy to misinterpret the challenges we face on our faith journey.

Our season of preparation is to do what it was designed to do: prepare us to overcome challenges and build our stamina for battle. Before David could fight Goliath, God sent him a lion and a bear to strengthen him (see 1 Samuel 17: 34-35). He had to know the enemy in a more diminutive form to build his faith to fight him as a giant. The same God that readied His son David is preparing you today.

God provides us with the proper tools to face our adversaries. We need the wisdom to know which tools to use, depending on the season. When we use the wrong weapon, we leave ourselves open, exposed, and defeated. God is coming to you today to remind you of what is in your arsenal (see Ephesians 6:13). Let's be ready to stand tall!

Sincerely,

Your friend

A Moment to Reflect

"Be sober, be vigilant; because your adversary the devil, as a roaring lion, walketh about, seeking whom he may devour."

1 Peter 5:8

Yesterday, we talked about the importance of maturity in personal development. Today, we'll look at how maturity and self-discipline go hand-in-hand. Self-discipline requires self-awareness, and today's scripture reminds us that being vigilant and clear-minded is key to overcoming challenges. In a world where there are many ways to avoid facing our problems, we need to stand firm and confront our battles. God encourages us to stay focused and not let distractions take over.

Do you know what vigilant means? It means always staying alert and on guard. When I was younger, my dad always instructed me to be aware of my surroundings. As a young girl, I didn't fully understand the importance, but as I matured, I realized the benefits of being alert. When you are alert, it gives you the advantage of knowing when danger is near. Being vigilant is not only important for physical safety but also for mental and emotional well-being. It helps us to identify and address potential threats or challenges before they become bigger problems. In today's fast-paced world, it's easy to get distracted and lose sight of what's important. That's why being vigilant is even more critical now than ever before.

Moreover, being vigilant also means being mindful of our own actions and how they impact others around us. It involves being conscious of the consequences of our choices and making responsible decisions. When we are vigilant, we are better equipped to navigate through life's challenges and make the most of the opportunities that come our way. Being vigilant is a valuable trait that we should all strive to cultivate. It keeps us safe and helps us to be more focused and effective in our daily lives. So the next time you hear someone talk about being vigilant, remember that it's not just about being watchful, but it's also about being aware, responsible, and proactive.

We have the tools to overcome the enemy and his tactics, but we need the Word of God to build a solid defense. The enemy's main objective is to destroy (see John 10:10), and we must be aware that he is always waiting and watching for his chance to strike – often when we least expect it. We must put in the effort during our downtime to be prepared for battle. As James 4:3 instructs, *"Resist the devil, and he will flee from you."* This means that we must be able to withstand the enemy's attacks. We can do that by studying the Word of God and learning to recognize God's voice to better understand the context of the scriptures we are reading and learning about. Otherwise, we may misinterpret situations, thinking that hardships are the enemy's doing and easy-going circumstances are God's blessings. However, God may cause trials and tribulation, and without the ability to discern, we may make poor choices based on our flawed assumptions.

The enemy knows his destination. My mom always said, "The enemy doesn't care about you because he knows where he will spend eternity." We all have a chance to determine where we will reside after death. Don't get caught up in what you think you know; instead, find the truth in God by spending time with Him. Our most admirable defense against Satan is the Word of God.

DAILY CHALLENGE

What barriers do you think cause people to be less vigilant in their lives? How have some of these barriers affected you or your current situation? God instructs us to wear His full armor; what is the most needed in your current position?

Day 4

Exploring the Depth of Anger: Beyond What Meets the Eye

Good morning, beautiful.

Do you like romantic movies? They are a hit or miss for me, but one that stands the test of time is *Titanic*. I love how beautiful Jack and Rose's love for each other was. However, the place that sparked their passion was also where they lost their passion. The crew of the Titanic made the mistake of underestimating a block of ice that turned out to be far more extensive and damaging than they had initially assumed.

Just like the iceberg in the movie *Titanic*, anger is only the tip of the iceberg. The real danger lies beneath, hidden from view. If we are not careful, our anger can grow into something unmanageable and wreak havoc in our lives. It's not that God is saying anger is inherently destructive, as we see in the Bible when Jesus threw the tables in the courtyard (see Matthew 21:12). Anger can be necessary, but we must not let it control us.

While anger is visible on the surface, it is driven by many other underlying factors, such as loneliness, guilt, shame, doubt, unforgiveness, pain, and trauma. God wants us to recognize the areas in our lives that need to change. We must look beyond our actions, decisions, and plans to see the actual damage that lies beneath. God works from the inside out because He knows that change must start from within to make an outward difference.

Sincerely,

Your friend

A Moment to Reflect

"How can you say to your brother, 'Brother, let me take the speck out of your eye,' when you yourself fail to see the plank in your own eye? You hypocrite, first take the plank out of your eye, and then you will see clearly to remove the speck from your brother's eye."

Luke 6:42 NIV

As followers of Christ, one of the most dangerous things we can do is to believe that we are without fault. In today's scripture, Jesus addresses the Pharisees, who are quick to judge others but fail to see the flaws within themselves. God is weary of seeing the walking dead. When we overlook the imperfections in our hearts, we are nothing more than lifeless bodies wandering the earth. We are no different from those we criticize as "sinners."

To know Christ is to adhere to His commandments, and the Bible says that the two most important commandments are to *"love God with all your heart and to love thy neighbor as thy self"* (Matthew 22:37). You can't love anyone if you aren't giving that same love to yourself. Most of us are ticking time bombs, and just like the Titanic, we are reaching the tip of destruction. God is telling you today to stop glorifying Him on the surface because the voids and dark places in our hearts are the part He is trying to get to. God was doing the same with the Sadducees and the Pharisees. Still, because they were so focused on the law, they could not understand the ministry of Jesus Christ, which was to fulfill the law. God doesn't want to know you at the peak of your anger but at the depths of your despair.

Understand that this world values titles and highlights our differences. Still, there is one thing that truly sets us apart: our relationship with Christ. The truth is that we all have struggles and hardships that we face. It's okay to not have it all together, because the Bible never speaks of us being perfect. When we open up about our struggles and are honest with ourselves, we create an opportunity for growth, healing, and addressing the underlying cause of our troubles. While it's great to study God's Word, building a relationship with Him and trusting that He will fulfill His promises is even better. Can you let Him see the plank that is in your eye?

DAILY CHALLENGE

Google "Angry Iceberg," then I want you to create your own map and identify the feelings that lie beneath the surface of your anger. When you can name it, you can tame it!

Day 5

Selfish Kind of Love

Good morning, beautiful.

According to the Oxford Dictionary, selfishness is described as "a person, action, or motive lacking consideration for others." In simpler terms, it's all about me, myself, and I. But what if I told you today that I want it to be all about you? At times, we tend to emphasize the difference between selfish and selfless actions without considering God's will. Under human jurisdiction, these terms can be negative. For example, "selfless devotion" is the definition of selflessness according to the Oxford Dictionary. However, sacrificing our own interests for the benefit of others can be manipulative, depending on who delivers the message.

What's real and concerning is that so many believers haven't experienced God's love. Love is an emotion, and when we teach against recognizing the feelings we have within, we reject what God wants to show us through His Spirit. Today, I want you to understand that taking the time to step back and reflect is essential. Remember that God will guide you through your wilderness, but first, He must remove "Egypt" from your life (see Exodus 14 - Joshua 1). Who you used to be cannot obtain what God has in store for you. Today's message will be delicate, but it will be necessary for the Christian community. God is calling for a change and for us to identify with Him, not just the idea of who He is.

Sincerely,

Your friend

A Moment to Reflect

"And as he journeyed, he came near Damascus: and suddenly there shined round about him a light from heaven: And he fell to the earth, and heard a voice saying unto him, Saul, Saul, why persecutest thou me? And he said, Who art thou, Lord? And the Lord said, I am Jesus whom thou persecutest: it is hard for thee to kick against the pricks."

Acts 9: 3-5

On the road to Damascus, God had to turn Paul inward to see the errors of his heart; this was a time for transformation. Many can look at Saul and assume he was an evil and bloodthirsty man. To the naked eye, that may be true. Saul was a man who took his orders seriously because he believed in his actions.[2] His actions reflected the Pharisees' mission to preserve what they considered true Judaism. The idea of Jesus threatened the Pharisees. Therefore, anyone who saw Jesus as the King of kings was considered an enemy under the law.

Saul lived a complicated life, because even though his actions were senseless and vile, they were selfless in nature. How so? Do you remember how we define selflessness? Selflessness is "an act of self-devotion." Saul wasn't serving his idea but that of the Pharisees; it was a group effort. One's cause merely determines the interpretation of actions. Today, we are divided in what and who we serve. We identify based on the groups we associate with, contributing to the filters through which we view life. Yet, we all believe in what we do, right?

One's idea of being selfish or selfless narrows down to the road traveled. It took Saul to be divided and desolate to experience transformation. Jesus modeled the way in which we should stand firm on the Word of God. We must choose to be indifferent to society's standards and traditions to walk in the way most pleasing to

Christ. Sometimes to the world this can be viewed as a selfish act, but when you understand the work of Christ then you will understand that everything He does is for the good of humankind. Jesus had to be indifferent to the law to fulfill the prophecy spoken in the Old Testament. The Pharisees knew that a King would arrive. Still, they missed Him because, like the Bible says, "*God's word is living and active. It is sharper than any two-edged sword and cuts as deep as the place where soul and spirit meet, the place where joints and marrow meet. God judges a person's thoughts and intentions*" (Hebrews 4:12 GW). It was hard for the Pharisees to accept God's truth and reality because they sought man's interpretation instead. God came for the lost and broken, and He loved us so much that He "*gave His only begotten Son*" to die on the cross for our sins (see John 3:16). Jesus had to go against the orders of this world to free us from the strongholds that kept us bound and stagnant.

When we walk in true selfishness, we act in ways to preserve our ideas and our mindset, no matter the cost. God is not divisive but inclusive. We live in a time when many denominations divide us from the truth. We all assume that we are "the better Christian," not realizing that we are falling right into the enemy's trap of deception. The truth is the Word of God. One Man had to stand indifferent to the law to fulfill the prophecy spoken in the Old Testament.

Putting yourself first because you need healing is not selfish but an act of service, or shall I say, selfless devotion. We, too, must be indifferent to the law to see the trueness of God's heart. As the dictionary says, being selfless is putting others' needs above your own, and who greater should we deny self for other than God? You see, I didn't say man but God. You are opening yourself to see God and what He desires you to do in His kingdom. Sometimes, in doing God's work, we may have to lack consideration of others, especially when those others go against the Spirit of God.

The Bible says that not everyone who says "Lord, Lord" will inherit the kingdom of God (see Matthew 7:21). The same message applies to you now. You must know the difference between "God told me" and "god told me." It may take a selfish act to separate yourself from naysayers, so don't be afraid to say yes to yourself and what you desire in your walk with Christ. God is sending you on the road to Damascus. He wants to transform you so you can know His ways and inherit the promise He has waiting for you.

DAILY CHALLENGE

What is God saying to you this morning through today's message? What are the areas He is asking you to pay closer attention to?

Week 2

The Tears You Don't See

A fun fact about me is that one of my favorite activities is sleeping! Yes, I love to sleep, and let me tell you, I can sleep anywhere. My friends in school used to laugh at me because whenever there was a quiet time in class, or maybe we had a 10-minute break during practice, I took that time to nap and did not feel an ounce of guilt about it.

Unfortunately, my love for sleep also became my way of isolating myself, as it helped me pass the time. Throughout high school, I was just sleeping away; those years were a blur because I didn't feel present. My goal was to survive. I thought life would get simpler when I started college, but my first year was a total bust. I went from an A and B student to someone who lost their life scholarship after the first year. I remember constantly feeling tired and not wanting to go to class. I did not have a passion or desire to complete my schoolwork or even study for tests. Everything during that time felt impossible.

Not only was I fighting to keep up with my schoolwork, but I also had this burning desire for companionship. I struggled with loneliness and felt as though no one understood me. I thought no one would ever desire to be with someone like me, and I had a warped view of myself and the people around me. I tried dating and throwing myself into relationships, hoping that if I loved enough, maybe that would fill the void in my heart.

I remember becoming so desperate to feel that I no longer cared about my value to save myself for marriage. I wanted to be in love and experience love, but I never felt good enough. So, I rationalized it in my mind that if I'm not good enough for someone to wait for me, what would it matter if I just gave it up? I figured that I wasn't saving myself for anything extraordinary. So, I decided to act off my emotions because I was looking for a spark I had lost and honestly don't even remember when the lights went out.

I made many mistakes due to feeling depressed and developed unhealthy attachments to people and food. I realized that sometimes pain doesn't always show in the form of tears, and some of our most profound battles are the ones we go through when others can't see.

Being depressed was an inward cry for help that wasn't always apparent to others. At times, I felt alone, abandoned, and afraid. I tried medication because my doctor prescribed it to me, and after a few weeks, I did see a change in my sleeping patterns. However, it didn't change my negative thoughts. I recognized that what I was experiencing wasn't just a depressed state but a severe void I could no longer try to fill alone. So I decided to flush every ounce of that medicine down the drain and looked to God.

One of the things that I have learned over time is that you don't have to utter words for God to hear you. God saw me at that moment, and before I knew His voice, He saw my heart. As Matthew 11:29 says, "Take my yoke upon you and learn of me." Being at a low point in my life forced me to look up and see God. I knew then that I needed someone or something more significant than what I was currently experiencing. God knew my mental state, and He still showed up and assured me He would bring me through.

That choice to turn to God was not easy, because the pain and misery I was experiencing held me captive, and it was hard to let go. It was an ugly reality until God indeed showed up in my life. I still remember it like it was yesterday; it was raining and super muggy outside, and I was driving down this curvy road. Alongside it were these beautiful white trees that I now know are called Bradford pear. Now, mind you, I have lived in this area for most of my life, and I can tell you these trees didn't just appear; it was like I saw life in HD on that day. Everything was bright and full of color and alive. It was as if I saw the breath of Jesus reviving what was once dead. My world was no longer dark from that day forward, and I knew God had finally freed me from depression.

Life didn't automatically become easy; there were moments when I still had to wrestle, but like Jacob, I held on and continued to hold on until God blessed me (see Genesis 32:22-32). By not letting go and giving up, God blessed me by being able to see His light. This moment is when I finally saw the God of Abraham, Isaac, and Jacob! No more just reading about Him or hearing about Him through other people's stories, because on that day, I saw Him He saw me, and our eyes met, and I haven't let go since.

God is telling you today that even in the silence of your tears, He hears and sees you! You are not alone; whatever you are going through, God is here to lift the burden off your life. He invites you to draw closer to Him and lay your worries and cares upon Him. I'm unsure if anyone has ever said these words to you, but know that *it's not your load to carry; you can let it go and walk away from whatever you feel is weighing you down.* God encourages us to lay our burdens at His feet. Today, God is calling you to a place of rest, but it's up to you to leave the baggage at the door.

Week 2

———∞———

Day 1

I Can't Just Pray About It

Good morning, beautiful.

A particular song that comes to mind this morning is "Take me to the King" by Tamela Mann. In my opinion, she spoke to every person's heart with this song. There are so many moments in life when it feels like we can't pray our way through, which can lead us to question our relationship with Christ. Within the Christian community, we put such a big emphasis on faith and praying, but what happens when we feel too weak to do anything?

Praying can open many doors, but it is important to know that prayer alone will not lead us to the answers we seek. God isn't only looking for words, but He is looking for actions. God wants our sacrifice and obedience above all else, and to do that, we must step outside of our fixed view of Christianity and realize that God is so much more than a few words. Don't believe me? God told the disciples, *"But when ye pray, use not vain repetitions, as the heathen do: for they think that they shall be heard for their much speaking." (Matthew 6:7).*

The Pharisees were men of many words and no actions. In Matthew 15:8, Jesus recognized that though they spoke many words, their hearts were far from Him. God is an action-filled God, and He knows the voids that are in your life. All that God wants is for you to give Him your heart!

Sincerely,

Your friend

A MOMENT TO REFLECT

"And in process of time it came to pass, that Cain brought of the fruit of the ground an offering unto the LORD. And Abel, he also brought of the firstlings of his flock and of the fat thereof. And the LORD had respect unto Abel and to his offering."

Genesis 4:3-4

Do you guys remember the story of Cain and Abel from when you were growing up? If you don't, let me give you a quick summary. Cain and Abel were brothers. Their parents were Adam and Eve. Cain and Abel delivered an offering to God, and God loved Abel's sacrifice but rejected Cain. So, being displeased and not wanting to change, Cain decided to kill his brother. The End.

This scripture is often used to talk about sacrifice and giving what is pleasing to the Lord. You know, giving up money, time, and material goods. This scripture is interpreted based on the current need in your church. However, today, our focus isn't on the church but on you. Looking back at Genesis 4: 3-4, it's evident that God preferred one offering over the other, and that's the end of the story, right? Well, no. It wasn't so much that one brother did better than the other, but one was focused on the Lord while the other was focused on himself.[3]

Cain was the oldest child of Adam and Eve. It isn't clear how far apart Cain and Abel were in age. However, I can almost imagine Adam wanting to show Cain everything because he was the firstborn. Adam knew how to give sacrifices to God. Undoubtedly, Adam taught his son this because he knew that this is how we commune with God. As a father, I am sure he wanted to equip his son with the necessary tools to have a relationship with Christ. For whatever reason, Cain rebelled, and his offering to Christ was a desire for God to be satisfied with the work of his hands.[4] In other words, "I should be blessed because I am a good person; I pray and read my Bible, so what about me? I am a better Christian than them." It sounds like vain repetition, but we all do it because it is easier to judge what we see.

Then we have Goody Two Shoes, Mr. Abel, who goes above and beyond in his offering to God. So we think, but in reality, that's not true. Abel didn't go above and beyond; he sacrificed what was necessary, and all it took was self-examination. Abel acknowledged that God was his Redeemer.

One recognized Christ, while the other recognized the works of man. God knows your heart and is aware of every desire you have. God isn't looking for mere repetition of words (see Matthew 6:7) but for someone who can recognize Him as their Lord and Savior. Only God can see what lies beneath the surface and judge us accordingly. Man sees when we pray, give, and "seek," but man cannot determine the day or hour we surrender. God respected Abel (see Genesis 4:4) because he didn't shy away from "the process of time" (see Genesis 4: 3). He gave all he had to what mattered the most: his relationship with God.

Daily Challenge

Why do you think God wasn't pleased with Cain's offering? By reflecting on your life, how would you describe the sacrifices you have made?

Day 2

A Beautiful Lie

Good morning, beautiful.

I want to start today with an affirmation. Please repeat after me! I am who God says that I am. Repeat it, "I am who God says I am!" No person's journey is the same, but trust and believe that God has a specific purpose for your life. However, we must remain vigilant of the enemy's cunning attempts to destroy our identity in Christ. You see, the enemy is a man of many schemes and plots, and his ultimate plan is to take us off course from what God has in store for us.

I once had someone advise me on how they overcame some of the destructive things the enemy whispered to them. They told me that journaling was their way of escape. They taught me that during times of feeling overwhelmed, your best defense is to write out the exact statements swirling in your mind. They told me they realized their beliefs didn't make sense after the thought was exposed. So, I had to give it a go; sure enough, they were right! The enemy can only use what he has in his arsenal, and he uses what he has to the best of his ability. The easiest way to attack God's people without fail is through our inner thoughts.

After all, the enemy doesn't know our future – he knows our past, which he uses to keep us in chains. Depression and anxiety result from the vault of lies we store that validate our feelings and perceptions of life. Still, it doesn't mean we must remain stuck. We must choose to know the truth today to begin dismantling the lies we have believed.

Sincerely,

Your friend

A Moment to Reflect

"Now the serpent was more subtil than any beast of the field which the LORD God had made. And he said unto the woman, Yea, hath God said, Ye shall not eat of every tree of the garden? And the serpent said unto the woman, Ye shall not surely die."

Genesis 3:1,4

The difference between truth and lies is how you phrase the sentence. It doesn't take much to omit a few words or neglect to give context to what you are trying to say. We all have the ability to manipulate information to suit our agenda. Some may justify it as a white lie, but the fact remains: a lie is still a lie, regardless of the speaker's intent.

Satan is a master manipulator, as demonstrated in the Garden of Eden when he twisted the truth to achieve his ends. He preys on human weakness, exploiting our sinful nature and appealing to our desire for pleasure and pride. However, Jesus countered Satan's tactics by relying on God's truth, as shown in Luke 4:3-12, where Christ was tempted in the same way we are today. Each time, Satan tried to deceive Jesus with a lie, but since Jesus is the Son of God and knows the truth, He was able to resist and be free.

We, too, hold the power to fight Satan and win. In 2 Corinthians 10:5-6, it says, *"Casting down imaginations, and every high thing that exalteth itself against the knowledge of God, and bringing into captivity every thought to the obedience of Christ; And having in a readiness to revenge all disobedience, when your obedience is fulfilled."* These are the instructions to reject the devil's thoughts, suggestions, or visions.

The enemy loves to tell stories because myths and fables are attractive. With the right flavoring, he can turn deception into a beautiful lie. That is no match for Christ, for John 1:1 says, "In the beginning was the Word, and the Word was with God, and the Word was God." If Christ lives in you, then today, God is showing you how to conquer the poison that has filled your mind, and He wants to empty your vault to supply you with His truths.

Daily Challenge

If you want freedom today, I bet you would see the omission of truth if you wrote down every lie the enemy ever told you. Let's take a moment to apply God's truth to the thoughts we have built up in our minds and see which can stand the test.

Day 3

Marionette

Good morning, beautiful.

I want to ask you a simple question: what controls you? Our environment, social circle, values, beliefs, and actions are the external forces that shape our daily decisions. Evaluating your surroundings and determining whether your options are conducive to your overall health and well-being is essential. These factors may not seem significant initially, but they could be the key to unlocking a sense of freedom once you identify what's holding you back.

My father always taught me that knowledge is power. Once you have it, no one can take it away from you. Understanding the factors influencing our behavior can lead us to reframe our thoughts and make healthier lifestyle choices. The Bible shows us how sin can spiral out of control and negatively impact our lives. James 1:13-15 warns us against temptation, stating that it is not from God and that yielding to our own lust leads to sin and ultimately to death.

Our flesh has limitations, and we often struggle to discern what is best for us. When we encounter spiritual warfare, connecting with God's presence becomes more challenging, though not impossible. As believers, we know the enemy cannot attack us directly, but he still roams and searches for a way in. Unfortunately, the entry point sometimes stems from within ourselves when we fail to recognize the negative influences that control our thoughts and actions. This can lead to self-destructive patterns in our lives.

Sincerely,

Your friend

A Moment to Reflect

"And Balaam answered and said unto the servants of Balak, If Balak would give me his house full of silver and gold, I cannot go beyond the word of the LORD my God, to do less or more"

Numbers 22:18

"And Israel abode in Shittim, and the people began to commit whoredom with the daughters of Moab"

Numbers 25:1

Money, power, and fame are the things that entice many people today. We all want to be the next influencer, world-renowned speaker, lottery winner, YouTube husband and wife. The list can go on and on. The question isn't so much if you could obtain it, but what is the cost of your riches? Balaam was a man that was devoted to himself, and he took opportunities to advance in life. So much so that when he was asked to curse God's people, he didn't miss the chance.

Even after several encounters with God, Balaam continued in his pursuit to curse God's people because he knew the reward that Balak was offering him. He chose riches over obedience. In Numbers 25:1, Balaam had the bright idea that instead of the curse being spoken on the people, he sought to allow the people of Israel to bring a curse upon themselves. He opened the door to sin and enticed the people so they could bring havoc to their own lives. His plan worked because the Israelite men fell victim to the enticement of the Moabite daughters. The Israelites were indulging in sexual immorality and false worship.

Understand that you are God's child, and when you entered His kingdom, you inherited the land of milk and honey. As the Bible says, *"no weapons formed against me shall prosper"* (Isaiah 54:17). The enemy will throw darts at you to divert you from God's plan. The Bible says that we are born into sin, and just like the Israelites who walked on uncharted territory, we share the same path. This world is sin, and the enemy is *"like a roaring lion waiting to see who he can devour"* (see 1 Peter 5:8-10), but we serve a God who has the power to control the enemy's hands. God has given us the freedom to be protected as we travel on uncharted land; we don't have to allow sin to enter our hearts. God wants to cut the strings that once controlled you and give you a life of substance and purpose (see Romans 6:18).

Here is an interesting fact about the Israelites in the book of Numbers. The Israelites had been wandering in the wilderness for a period of time, until God commanded them to journey to the land of the Canaanites. This marked their initial encounter with false religion.[5] As we know, every action taken by God has intention and purpose. Don't you know that God sent them there at that time because He had planned for the Israelites to eliminate the false worship and practices that were happening?[6] This is an example to show you that there is a reason for your current destination. But are you focused enough on understanding your purpose in this season or are you more focused on the darts and schemes planted by the enemy?

There are check points throughout this journey, and we don't know when or where they will happen; trust and believe there will be moments to test your faith and your obedience. God is working to rid you of the things that can control you and the vulnerable areas that could be easily manipulated. If you do not spend time building a relationship with Christ, you will not know how to take charge and overcome life's mishaps or pitfalls.

DAILY CHALLENGE

I want you to create a control map; below is an example of what it should look like. After you have created yours, please write the barriers that affect your ability to focus on what you can control. What are the things causing you to fumble as you progress in this journey?

BEYOND MY CONTROL

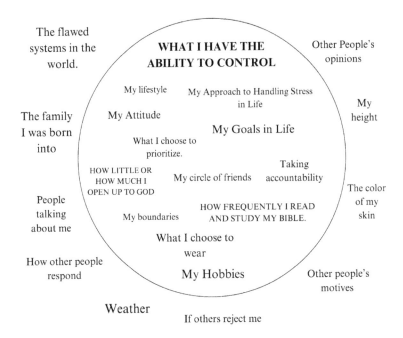

Day 4

Dry Bones Can Come Alive.

Good morning, beautiful.

I have this beautiful plant at home called the nerve plant, which is my absolute favorite. I love to refer to her as Ms. Dramatic because this plant will appear lifeless if it doesn't love the current conditions or needs to be watered. It doesn't take much for this plant to go from thriving to limp, and it will appear lifeless and near death until you give it what it needs.

I, too, once felt like this plant, limp and near death because of my depression. It wasn't until God came and changed my condition that I felt alive again. He restored me and allowed me to see life. When we suffer from mental illness, it can feel like we are in this vault—jam-packed with our fears and past trauma experiences. You may feel as though life will always be like this, and there is no way things can change. It's almost as if you are chained and forced to live with a broken heart and mind.

The beauty of the nerve plant is that once it is cared for correctly, it's strong, sturdy, and whole. It stretches towards the sun, and it stands tall. God is leading you to the place to experience being cared for so you can live! He is bringing life to you so it can flow through you. To achieve this experience, we first must recognize that we need help, and instead of running around trying to find solutions we think will work, we need to go to God and allow Him to lead us to the correct resource. He knows what we need and when we need it! That's a promise.

Sincerely,

Your friend

A Moment to Reflect

"And it came to pass, as they were burying a man, that, behold, they spied a band of men; and they cast the man into the sepulchre of Elisha: and when the man was let down, and touched the bones of Elisha, he revived, and stood up on his feet."

2 Kings 13:20-21

According to the Oxford Dictionary, there are several ways to define the word dead. One way is "no longer alive," which we all know to be someone who is no longer living. A few other definitions of dead are "having lost sensation, numb; lacking emotion, sympathy, or sensitivity; characterized by a lack of activity or excitement; no longer current, relevant, or important." As you can see, the word dead means several things. However, if something is dead, it isn't lost. Lost is not knowing where you are and how to get to a place. If something is lost, no one knows where it is.

You are not lost, and I know firsthand how the enemy can come in and make you feel unwanted, unlovable, and worthless. When we feel dead inside, we automatically assume that there is no way God can revive us again. Or worse, we think life is better after death, like maybe that's the solution. It must mean that death is our only option to stop the pain or be free of our internal voids. I am here to tell you that death is not the option God wants for you! In the Bible, we hear about Lazarus, Jesus, and an unnamed man being raised from the dead. All these stories prove a point: that we can rise from the dead. But what about when death isn't a physical concept but an emotional and spiritual one? Can the same method be applied? The answer is yes!

Remember how I provided different definitions of the word dead at the beginning? You see, we must understand the tricks of the enemy. He only reminds you of one death, involving being completely lifeless and buried in the ground. If the dictionary can have several definitions to define one word, don't you think that God does as well? The Bible says in Ephesians 2:1, "And you hath he quickened, who were dead in trespasses and sins."

God tells us that there is more than one way to be dead, and (V.1) teaches us of the spiritual death we experience when we are walking in sin and the ways of this world. Some of us have been spiritually dead for a long time, and we have grown accustomed to our lifestyles and neglected to realize our spiritual time of death. Jesus died (physically) on the cross so He could come back and give us the spiritual gift of the Holy Spirit.

On the cross, God knew even then the agonizing pain His children would one day experience as they move through life numb and lifeless. He knew they would need His Spirit to live in them so they could experience the supernatural powers of being revived and awakened (see Acts 2:38).

DAILY CHALLENGE

Can you name the areas in your life that need reviving? How can you make room for the Holy Spirit to enter your life? What lifestyle changes do you need to make to see God's presence?

Below are a few scriptures to reference,
as they assure us of the Holy Spirit:

"What? know ye not that your body is the temple of the Holy Ghost which is in you, which ye have of God, and ye are not your own?"

1 Corinthians 6:19

But ye shall receive power, after that the Holy Ghost is come upon you: and ye shall be witnesses unto me both in Jerusalem, and in all Judaea, and in Samaria, and unto the uttermost part of the earth."

Acts 1:8

"But the Comforter, which is the Holy Ghost, whom the Father will send in my name, he shall teach you all things, and bring all things to your remembrance, whatsoever I have said unto you."

John 14:26

Day 5

Inspired by a True Story

Good morning, beautiful.

Each one of us has a story to tell. I promise that no matter how life looks, we all struggle with our demons. The beauty of God is that He doesn't choose favorites or judge us based on where we have come from. He doesn't judge us by our mistakes, either. God sees us for who we will become in His kingdom.

I remember the first time I was told about speaking to other singles, and I wanted to run from that calling. I thought there couldn't be a good enough reason to write about my experiences, let alone talk about them. Then, God showed me that there is power in my testimony. God sees your heart today, and just as He uses my testimony to touch you, He wants this to be a ripple effect.

Remember that you matter. You may feel insignificant in a big world, but we serve a God that has overcome this world. There is power in your words today. One day, your story will inspire others because your story has the power to make a difference in the world, and your perseverance can inspire others to do the same. Praying for your spouse isn't just about being married, but it's the inner work that God is doing in your life that will forever impact those around you.

Sincerely,

Your friend

A Moment to Reflect

"But sanctify the Lord God in your hearts: and be ready always to give an answer to every man that asketh you a reason of the hope that is in you with meekness and fear:"

1 Peter 3:15

My mom always said you won't look like what you have been through when you walk in Christ. We will face trials and setbacks in life. Still, God's favor is on you through every tribulation as He prevents you from deteriorating in the storm. He protects our youth because someone from the outside will question how you have been able to overcome life's adversities. There will always be someone somewhere watching you and learning from you.

God's goal is to shine His light through us so others may experience His glory. When we go through trials and tribulations, it can be easy to lose sight of God's plan for our lives. However, it's important to remember that our struggles are not in vain. Just as gold is refined through fire, our character is strengthened and refined through the challenges we face. Our experiences can be used to encourage and uplift others who may be going through similar situations.

It may not seem like it now, but trust and believe you have a testimony to share. God knows that a new generation of people can benefit from you just as we have benefited from those in our past and the many stories we have read throughout the Bible. God called us all to be purposeful in Him, and that purpose isn't built overnight. Yet, we all have something to add to advance the kingdom of Christ, and I want you to spend time telling your story. Get a pen and some paper, and let's get started!

DAILY CHALLENGE

Tell me about the times you've experienced or seen God's presence in your life. Let this be the beginning of an inspiring story!

Week 3

The Obvious Villain

So, to all my TikTok junkies, I know you have seen the trend that goes something like this "Am I the villain? I'm not the villain." It's funny because it states the obvious: Maybe I am the problem, but who in their right mind wants to admit that? I'll go first! I will confess this week, and I'm sure you have figured it out; I admit today that I was the villain!

Once upon a time, in the early stages of my journey as a single person, I experienced the unimaginable and was hit with the jealousy bug. This was worse than any sickness I've ever experienced because it almost stole my joy, relationships, peace, and sanity. I would always hear that *the enemy comes to steal, kill, and destroy* (John 10:10). Little did I know that the enemy made a campground right in the middle of my heart. He hit me with the most potent offense that turned my life upside down.

My experience with jealousy is painful to remember, but at the same time, it reminds me of God's grace and mercy. Despite my negative behaviors, the person my jealousy was directed toward had such a loving and forgiving spirit that she accepted me when it was time for me to right my wrongs. I want to shout out to that person— thank you, sister, for not dismissing me or holding a grudge against me. Your act of kindness was the warmth that I needed to experience.

It is a daily reminder of how great and loving our Father in Heaven is to His children.

I don't want to hold anything back this morning because truth be told, we must start facing our demons to win this fight, even if the enemy is ourselves. So, I want to share my story with you, and I hope that as you are reading this, you realize that you aren't alone. I pray that you can reconcile with those you hurt due to jealousy. Here is my story:

I began praying for God to send me a husband in my early twenties. I was sure that once I made my request known to God, there would be a quick turnaround, and I would soon be walking down the aisle with my one true love. Well, to my surprise, that didn't happen. A year went by, and then two and then three, and slowly but shortly, I felt my time clock just ticking away. I remained hopeful that I would have at least met the person I was destined to spend the rest of my life with by the time I graduated from college. Well, reality quickly set in because little did I know my younger sister would beat me to the punch. Not only did she meet someone, but he was around my age, which seemed utterly unfair.

To cope with my emotions, I rationalized the situation by saying, "She's still in school, she's younger than me, and the relationship may not even last." All these thoughts ran through my mind except for the obvious option, "This could actually be her husband." Spoiler alert: it wasn't too long after they met that they got engaged and began planning their wedding. I remember the day my brother-in-law proposed to my sister. We were celebrating my parents' 25th wedding anniversary. When I saw him get down on one knee and everyone was in awe at what was taking place at this beautiful moment, I remember sitting there. The first thought that popped into my head was, "This is supposed to be me!" The ugly part behind all of this was that others noticed my jealous spirit. They saw clear as day the utter disgust I had on my face. When I should have been celebrating with my sister, I was off in the back, full of rage. I had to be coached by my older brother to go forward and congratulate her. Immediately, I had to paint this smile on my face, but deep down inside, I felt like I was being torn into two pieces.

During the event, to make matters worse, this lovely, kind lady tried to encourage me by saying, "Oh, don't worry, sweetie, my sister is still praying for her husband, and she's in her forties." I don't know about you all, but my blood was boiling then. I'm sitting there thinking, "How in the world was that even slightly motivating." I mean, here I am in my early 20s, and this lady tells me that her sister, who is in her 40s, almost 50, is still praying for her husband!!! I almost lost it, but luckily, I held it together.

After that night, I went into a downward spiral, and before I knew it, I was causing a lot of havoc within my home. I couldn't even be a part of the special moments of helping my sister plan for her big day because the thought of being around anything dealing with a wedding was too much to handle. I didn't want to feel this way, and I was in constant turmoil with myself in my fight to hide it from everyone. The part that made it worse was that despite my negative feelings, my sister was still there for me. So much so that when I started dating, she encouraged me because she knew how badly I wanted to be married despite my feelings toward her.

I had to learn the hard and obvious truth that I was neither perfect nor better than the next person, all because I chose to wait on God. This was a make-it-or-break-it point for me because, for the first time since beginning my prayer, I was tested on how much I trusted God to bless me with a husband. God revealed through jealousy that my feelings towards my sister were never about her getting married. It showed that the root of my behavior was how I viewed her compared to myself. I was jealous of the fact that she was free to be who she was and how she met someone who accepted her, whereas I struggled so much with low self-esteem and being a people pleaser that I spent the first 21 years of my life morphing myself to be liked instead of being me! I was jealous because, unlike my sister, I held so much of my feelings in, and no one around me knew the internal wars I was fighting. At this moment, I had no choice but to act out because this wasn't something I could keep bottled inside.

God used that season to show me the obvious villain—myself. God brought out some deep, hidden places I had tucked away and avoided for a long time because I didn't think it was necessary to address them. God used a horrid time in my life to reveal His inner beauty. No one in their right mind wants to be told that they have a hateful and ugly heart, but that revelation led me closer to God. God had to show me to me just as He is showing you to you. He is opening your eyes to the areas that may not have been detrimental in past relationships, but if not dealt with, they will ruin His plans for you.

This week, we're dedicating our efforts to recognizing our negative tendencies and working towards overcoming them. With empathy, care, and passion, we can silence our inner beast and make positive changes that will bring us closer to God.

Day 1

Learn You Honestly

Good morning, beautiful.

There is a reason why we choose to indulge in earthly things. It feeds our appetite, and it allows us to be distracted from the issues happening in our lives. No one wants to be present with themselves because it can reveal the ugly parts we don't want to acknowledge. However, to move into the season, God calls us into, we must learn ourselves honestly. What that means is to see our strengths but also to see our areas of weakness.

To learn you honestly is when you show up for yourself every day despite the discomfort of learning who you are. So many people are trying to be like everyone else because of trends and the fear of missing out (FOMO). If we go back to the beginning of creation, when God made Adam and Eve, He created them specific to their purpose and calling. If we are all trying to be like each other, how can we walk in the purpose that God has for our lives? It will no longer be the fear of missing out because we will miss out on OUR blessing.

The only way to learn ourselves honestly is for us to rip off the Band-Aids and let the wounds show. God is in the season to give you a new experience so He can reveal His truth to you. Can you learn enough to withstand the trial?

Sincerely,

Your friend

A Moment to Reflect

"And it came to pass, when they were come, that he looked on Eliab, and said, Surely the LORD's anointed is before him. But the LORD said unto Samuel, Look not on his countenance, or on the height of his stature; because I have refused him: for the LORD seeth not as man seeth; for man looketh on the outward appearance, but the LORD looketh on the heart."

1 Samuel 16:6-7

Taking your request to God for a spouse was not easy, and you deserve credit for wanting to pursue a godly relationship. What I say next may sting a bit, but I must tell you that just because you serve Jesus doesn't mean blessings will be handed out. If anything, God is looking for your willingness to endure trials. Your blessing is your testimony; that is what He wants to show this world! So many Christians avoid conflict, and they avoid anything that requires true pressure to be applied to their circumstances. God is not trying to hurt you but to rid you of deadly things in your life. Blessing is not what I can get, but it's about what I had to go through to get it and whether it was worth the ask.

Just like Jesse, we attempt to deliver what we consider to be the best parts of ourselves. We assume that our appearances are the key to opening opportunities. The truth is God does not judge worth the same way man judges it, and our shortcomings are when we don't understand what it requires to be next in line to be blessed in life. Jealousy is explained as wanting what others have or what you can't have at that moment. Before entering this season of waiting, you began praying for your spouse, and I am sure you were not expecting this wait to be long. So, it is natural to feel upset when everyone on your timeline is getting engaged or getting married, and it feels that there are no good prospects in your direction. You are probably wondering how in the world it is not your turn when you have been devoted to waiting.

If you continue reading 1 Samuel 16, you will see that God honored the man who remained devoted in his season of waiting. Samuel had to go down the line of Jesse's sons, and in the end, the son who didn't seem qualified was qualified. Man makes mistakes, but God doesn't, and He knows your heart. So, if God reveals specific areas of your life that need to be managed, trust that God is readying your heart to receive His gift for you. It won't be too soon or too late, but it will be on time.

DAILY CHALLENGE

The most rewarding aspect of learning is discovering your own inner strength. Ask yourself: What aspects of my life am I neglecting to confront due to fear? Acknowledging these areas can be the first step in unlocking your full potential.

Day 2

The Practice of Self-Restraint: Do Not Give in to Your Own Desires

Good morning, beautiful.

Do you guys remember the show *Wife Swap* that used to come on television? In each episode, two families would trade places to see what life was like with a different mom in the home. The purpose of the show was to entertain curiosity. It allowed people to see if life was greener on the other side. Most of the wives on the show preferred to be with their own families. They learned that what they had was better than what they imagined. Our curiosity can open the door for imaginative thoughts that can lead us to wonder what life would be like if we experienced something different or finally had the thing we were praying for.

The enemy can overshadow our thoughts, so we see life only through negative lenses. We create this mindset by thinking everything will work out once we receive what we desire. The truth is that the grass isn't greener on the other side, but it is where you water it. Seeing everyone around you getting engaged, married, and having babies is hard. However, if we aren't careful, we can become covetous of our friends and loved ones because we will begin to envy what they have. Jealousy is rooted in fear; it is your job this morning to know your fears and be honest with God. God wants to know this side of you just as much as He wants to know the parts of you that are pleasing and good.

Sincerely,

Your friend

A Moment to Reflect

"Trust in the LORD with all thine heart;
and lean not unto thine own understanding.
In all thy ways acknowledge him,
and he shall direct thy paths."

Proverbs 3:5-6

Do you know what it means to trust with your whole heart? It's a level of trust that is unwavering, undoubtful, and without fear. Trusting in God takes a lot of courage, and we must consciously depend on Him. Take, for instance, a chair; you trust it will hold you up and support you so much that when you sit in it, you assume you will not fall. That is the kind of trust we must have in God. Knowing who He is and what He is all about, we must understand that we will trust Him to support us no matter what we encounter in life.

When we are covetous towards our neighbors, we confuse what we know to be true with what we feel to be true. There is a reason why God commanded us that we should not covet (see Exodus 20:17). It is because it is rooted in self-desires. When we are focused more on self, we suffer from the natural consequence of disregarding God's law. Trust me when I say what you think you want versus what you actually receive will be very different. From personal experience, walking in the way of covetousness leads you down a darker path of loneliness, feeling unfulfilled and desperate.

When we follow God's Word and we trust in Him, we no longer have the desire to want what is not ours to begin with. If you walk in a spirit of covetousness, you neglect your responsibilities (see 1 Thessalonians 3:6-15). God attached an assignment to you; every assignment has a distinctive request. When you focus on what others have, you are missing the opportunity to adhere to the assignment God has assigned to you. This is how the enemy traps and chains us down so that we never receive our blessings. No one on the face of the earth is exempt from being molded and pruned. We all acquire specific edits from God, but we cannot continue judging ourselves and comparing steps with our neighbors.

DAILY CHALLENGE

Read Psalms 119: 33-40. We all struggle with wanting the riches of life, but God teaches us in these scriptures to depart from worldly things, because happiness is not equated to the abundance of things you may have in your possession. It is time to clean house, so I encourage you this morning to allow the Holy Spirit to guide you and show you the hardened parts of your heart. Write what the Spirit reveals to you so you may be more aware of the areas God wants to change within you.

Day 3

The Making of a Great Warrior

Good morning, beautiful.

I know it may feel like you are in this constant place of warring within yourself. That's the fight between your flesh and your spirit. It will feel like a battle, and there will be moments when you feel defeated, but I want you to keep fighting. You are a warrior, and to be a great one, you have to know that this place you are in is not forever. A warrior is someone who never gives up and continues to fight to protect themselves. They also know the importance of possessing the skill set and strength to conquer their enemies and win!

Today is about winning and being the strong warrior God has called you to be. The things that we are warring against, God has given us the skills and the strength to overcome, but now He needs us to learn how to protect ourselves and to fight as if we are fighting for our last breath. That takes courage; when you have courage, you will have the willpower to keep fighting and pushing.

These obstacles in your path will not overtake you, nor will you continue speaking negative things about your life. You will not live in constant regret, because this morning you are choosing to wage war against every enemy in hell. Today, you are taking the step to take back what belongs to you and reclaim peace of mind! So, hold on and know that your journey is far from being over. God is giving you the desire to fight. Are you ready?

Sincerely,

Your friend

A Moment to Reflect

"As it is my eager expectation and hope that I will not be at all ashamed, but that with full courage now as always Christ will be honored in my body, whether by life or by death."

Philippians 1:20 ESV

Something about those medieval-based movies and television shows gives us an up close and personal experience of warring back then. Many great men fought to honor their lord or king and fellow compatriots. They were dedicated and valorous men. They were the epitome of a knight in shining armor! They fought with a purpose and were willing to die for their cause.

It took courage and strength to be in the midst of other men wielding their swords and fighting to live. To face death so close, I can only imagine the pride and honor most of these men felt when they survived and celebrated another day on earth, another moment to spend with their loved ones, and another opportunity to serve their lord or king and fight for causes that represented their country.

As children of God, we must have a purpose for who we will serve. Either we are going to fight to live or fight to die. God says in His Word that we must die to this flesh daily (see Romans 8:13). This means we must rid ourselves of the potent things in our lives that are causing us to wilt away. You have to see value within yourself; to do that, you must constantly fight against anything that may lead you toward destruction.

God clarifies the kind of people who will not inherit the kingdom of God, which includes fornicators, idolaters, adulterers, effeminate, abusers, thieves, covetous, drunkards, revilers, or extortioners (1 Corinthians 6: 9-10). God has called us into a season of fighting, and in doing so, He is raising up a valiant warrior who desires and respects God's kingdom and will fight to protect it at all costs.

You are facing spiritual battles now because the enemy is after your position in the kingdom. He will use whatever and whomever to get you off your mark. Walking in things that are not pleasing to God weakens your defense. So, when you hold on to grudges or have anger towards your brother or sister, you are allowing the enemy to gain traction in your life.

Remember, most battles are won by those who believe in the vision of what's to come. They don't run at the sight of a sword or men charging at them; instead, they stand in a firm position because they believe in the vision of what is to come by being victorious. So they stand to fight "whether it be by life or by death" (Philippians 1:20).

DAILY CHALLENGE

Read Philippians 1:19. God promised to deliver you from your situation, but in the way He wants to do it. We have to purpose in our hearts to fight for God's causes, even if that means we have to war against ourselves. This morning, please write down how jealousy or other ungodly spirits have robbed you of your joy.

Day 4

Probable Cause

Good morning, beautiful.

Have any of you ever baked or cooked any meals? If yes, then you know that every recipe will require its own list of ingredients. Making something delicious takes time and work but can also leave you a mess. So, out of curiosity to all my master chefs, how many ingredients does it take to make a mess? Well, I will give you the answer. It only takes one. One ingredient can turn a polished kitchen into utter disarray, just like one ingredient can potentially turn our lives upside down.

We are all struggling with something, and life doesn't make it easy to pinpoint where the problem lies. Have you ever heard that saying, "Causation is not correlation"? It means that just because two things exist, it doesn't mean they affect each other, but all behaviors have meaning. So, even though it may be challenging to identify the infected areas, our circumstances can open our eyes, and we can begin the journey toward change.

Jealousy is what we see, but it took many ingredients to get us to that place. Maybe you experienced one too many rejections, not feeling loved or wanted, struggling with insecurities, and feeling betrayed. Too many occurrences of anything can lead you down a path of destruction. God wants to clean up the mess, and He is reaching His hands out to you this morning, so you don't have to endure this challenge alone. It's time to clean up, so let's get to it!

Sincerely,

Your friend

A Moment to Reflect

"And as they did eat, he said, Verily I say unto you,
that one of you shall betray me."

Matthew 26:21

During His last Passover, Jesus is sitting amongst the disciples, and He reveals to them all that someone at the table will betray Him. I can only imagine how quiet and still it may have gotten for a second as each pondered and questioned if Jesus was talking about them. Each took a full observation of themselves, yet no one came forward. The villain in the room at the Passover feast was Judas Iscariot.

Judas was a man that was very present in all Jesus did on the earth. He witnessed miracles, heard various teachings, and saw Jesus raise people from the dead. He had front-row tickets to see God's works, yet he still betrayed Jesus for thirty pieces of silver. So, it is not enough to say, "Well, God, if You work this one thing out for me, then surely, I will believe." Judas saw, and it still wasn't enough for him to submit to God and be a true follower of Jesus Christ.

The thing that we often miss when it comes to Judas is that he didn't become a man of betrayal overnight. In time, he gave way to the enemy because he continued to walk in his way (see John 12:6). Satan purposed in Judas's heart that he would betray Jesus (see Luke 22:3-4; John 13:2; John 13:27). Judas had a lot of ingredients that he stopped observing, and soon he left behind one cracked egg here, and then he left a trail of breadcrumbs there. Before you knew it, he had a trail of waste lying at his feet.

We don't often like the idea of our choices having consequences, but they do. Judas had a choice, just as we have a choice. God is allowing you to turn away from the evil that has consumed you. He asks you to closely examine the ingredients shaping your life to see which ones are causing the mess. Life is all about what you make it to be, and my grandmother always told me that she cooks because it brings people together. That's the outcome God wants us to have when we are walking in His Way.

DAILY CHALLENGE

Every behavior is a reflection of something within us. Take a moment to reflect on your current actions and what they might be telling you about yourself. Consider listing all the ingredients causing turmoil in your life. How can these imperfections lead you to discover a new understanding of Jesus?

Day 5

A Mother's Advice

Good morning, beautiful.

Have you ever heard the saying, "Kill them with kindness"? I remember growing up, my mom always told my siblings and me that when people mistreat us, instead of seeking revenge, we should show kindness. I used to think that I would be so kind to people that it would cause them to feel so guilty for mistreating me that they would regret the day they ever hurt me. I believed this to be true until I realized I was unkind. My sister took my mom's advice, and through her acts of kindness, she showed me a level of compassion that I did not deserve.

I realized that her kindness didn't make me feel guilty for how I treated her, but it made me feel remorseful. The difference between guilt and remorse is that guilt leads to destructive tendencies, whereas remorse leads to constructive actions. Being shown kindness allowed me to see and experience God's love, and I could apologize to my sister for my behaviors and take ownership of my actions that caused her pain.

Today is about realizing the importance of grace and forgiveness. I pray that God heals your heart from the pain you have endured that caused you to be unkind to others. In due time, I hope you are allowed to right your wrongs and be shown kindness so that you can experience God's unwavering love for you.

Sincerely,

Your friend

A Moment to Reflect

"But I say unto you which hear, love your enemies,
do good to them which hate you, Bless them that curse you,
and pray for them which despitefully use you."

Luke 6:27-28

Not too long ago, I had a situation that involved some people mistreating me as well as those around me, and there were many times I wanted to treat them the way they were treating me! Luckily, a friend reminded me that even though someone has hurt you, they are still God's children. Man, when I tell you, this advice stung me to the core. I had to be reminded that you can't conquer evil with evil. God is love and reigns on the "just and unjust" (Matthew 5:45).

Hear me when I say it takes a special person to love their enemies, yet that is the command God has instructed us to do in His Word. Not everyone will heed this message, which will be okay. The reason is God still has His foot soldiers, and for those who will hear, God will give you the strength to do what your enemy can't, which is to love and be kind. God modeled this act of kindness through Jesus. During Jesus' ministry on earth, there was a considerable threat of religious persecution. As many of you know, the Pharisees and the Sadducees did not take to Jesus' ministry very well. Every time you looked, they tried to capture and persecute Him. Yet, Jesus still commands us to love our enemies, speak well to those who curse us, and pray for those who have wronged us.

God tells us to love and be kind to one another because He knows how important that act can be to His children. When we are kind, we walk in the likeness of God. Don't you know that kindness is one of the 12 Fruits of the Spirit God tells us to have (see Galatians 5)? So, know that God is not calling you to bear a useless skill. If He has been preaching kindness to you, trust it is for a reason. The goal is for the people on this earth to see God, and the way to do that is we have to model it for others so they can experience God's way. This in turn might encourage them to "taste and see" (see Psalms 34:8) for themselves.

DAILY CHALLENGE

Read Luke 6: 31-36. Loving those who have hurt us can be hard, but God wants to remind you of the reward of practicing the Golden Rule this morning! Think back to the ones who have shown you a level of kindness you did not deserve. How was that person's action impactful in your life?

Week 4

Effort is Wisdom's Door Key

It's important to remember that setbacks and disappointments are a natural part of life. However, it's how we choose to respond to them that shapes our future. Rather than dwelling on what didn't work out, we must focus on what we can learn from the experience and how we can grow from it. In the end, we may not end up exactly where we thought we would, but if we trust in God's plan, we will ultimately end up exactly where we are meant to be.

How so, you may ask? For example, I never imagined getting to a place where I could handle heartache and realize that my world wasn't ending. It took time for me to get to that place, but after trusting God and seeing how He showed up in so many other areas of my life, my trust in Him was stronger than the disappointments. I realized that I am strong and resilient. It wasn't by my strength but through God's I discovered that letting go of something that wasn't meant for me allowed me to make space for the things that were. For the first time in my life, I chose God's way over my own, and I decided to protect what was more precious to me: my relationship with God.

Although it wasn't easy, I learned to lean on God during this difficult time. I spent more time in prayer and reflection and started to see things from a different perspective. I realized that God had a plan for my life far greater than anything I could have imagined.

Looking back, I am grateful for the experience because it allowed me to grow stronger in my faith and develop a deeper relationship with God. I know that I can trust God to guide me through whatever challenges come my way. And I am confident that He will continue to use my experiences to shape me into the person He created me to be.

I always heard that what is for you will be for you, and to mature in this walk, you begin to understand that when things fall apart, you learn that it wasn't about you, but the purpose of that person has been completed. I firmly believe that people come into our lives for a reason, and they leave for a reason. If you find yourself at a crossroads this morning, take comfort that this week is all about letting go of things that no longer serve a purpose in our lives. Trust the bigger picture and believe that God has something significant in store for you. Will you choose to walk in God's wisdom over everything else? Let's find out together this week!

Day 1

Do you Remember the Manna?

Good morning, beautiful.

I want us to take a trip down memory lane; what can you recall as you reminisce about your happiest memory? I want to get your brain juices flowing this morning because when we go through trials, we can get lost and forget that not every day or every moment of our lives is terrible. Focusing on positive experiences and surrounding ourselves with positive people can increase our resilience and our ability to manage life stressors.

The lenses we view life through are crucial for how we see and experience God. God lives in the good and the bad, and to encourage us, God sends reminders to help us remember who He is. I will never forget the time I stood in line at Chipotle, and I remember just saying to God, "It would be nice for someone to pay for my meal today." Not thinking that it would happen, I go through the process of ordering, and as I am standing at the cash register, a gentleman behind me just says to the cashier, "Hey, put her food on my order." This moment allowed me to see that God does indeed hear my request.

God sends us provisions, just as He did to the Israelites in the wilderness. God wants us to know Him and not forget His promises as we hike through the valley. We must remember the manna because that is how God shapes our view of the world. He reminds us that there is hope in the unknown.

Sincerely,

Your friend

A Moment to Reflect

"And when the Children of Israel saw it, t
hey said one to another, it is Manna."

Exodus 16:15

There is always this big question about what manna is. Some focus on the taste and describe it as wafers made with honey.[7] Others focus on its appearance and say it is a round, white substance like a coriander seed (see Numbers 11:7). Both provide great descriptions. Still, the most essential detail of manna is that it was not a naturally occurring substance.[8] There were no human measures used to supply this food. It was all God! God was the supplier and made it so that the Israelites had to rely on Him every morning (see Exodus 16:13-22). God orchestrated this occurrence to build their trust and dependence on Him rather than on man.

Just as God worked on the Israelites, God is doing the same within us. God provides us with opportunities to grow in our trust and faith in Him. How, you may be asking? Well, let's take a moment and recall a few things. What did God do when you didn't know how things would work in your favor? How did God comfort you when you cried yourself to sleep at night? How has God encouraged you when a relationship ended and you wanted to give up? These are all examples of moments God uses in our life to supply His manna. God knows what you need, how, and when you need it.

The Israelites had to collect what they could eat every morning. God didn't allow it to fill over into the next day because He wanted to teach them that yesterday's blessings would not do for today. God wants you not to give up on hope, but He knows that He must work this trust muscle out, and therefore, He is conditioning you to seek

Him every day. This allows us to see our Father's will and commune with Him.

I know that this place you are in is probably uncomfortable because it's unfamiliar. I encourage you to trust God anyhow. God would not have allowed you to progress to where you are now if He hadn't believed you could handle this season. We don't always know what will come, but we know Who will provide. Manna in Hebrew is translated as "what is it."[9] Not even the Israelites recognized the bread that God provided for them. God was trying to teach the people to break away from the conditions of their flesh and pay attention to the needs of their souls. God is feeding you this morning with His bread. It doesn't look or taste like anything you have ever had, and that is for a reason. God is leading you to acquire a new and stronger taste in Him. Are you ready to try manna?

Daily Challenge

What's your manna story? How did it allow you to grow closer to God? If you don't feel you have a story yet, what can you do to improve how you commune with God?

Day 2

The Body's Engine Room

Good morning, beautiful.

As you prepare for today's reading, I want you to put your first and middle fingers on the side of your neck. Press lightly to feel your pulse. Do you feel your heart's steadiness and strength effortlessly working to ensure that your body receives blood and oxygen? You may not see it in action, but you can feel the fist-sized muscle that sits in the middle of your chest at work. Just take another moment and be present with your heart this morning.

Your heart is such an important body member that you cannot live without it. That is why God instructs us to protect it always. Proverbs 4:23 NIV says, "Above all else, guard your heart, for everything you do flows from it." Our hearts are not like any other organs in our bodies. Our hearts are muscles that needs to be strengthened every day. Just like we go to the gym to build muscle to be lean and fit, we must apply the same methods to strengthen our hearts.

The work that we do in our walk with God is to strengthen us from within. For the body to function, our hearts pump blood and send oxygen to the needed organs. Spiritually, our hearts reflect who we are. This morning, we are going to the spiritual gym and focusing on building our spiritual muscles to continue the journey God has carved out for us. Just a reminder to know that you are a living and breathing being, place those two fingers on your neck, and remember that your heart beats so you can live!

Sincerely,

Your friend

A Moment to Reflect

"Above all else, guard your heart, for everything you do flows from it."

Proverbs 4:23 NIV

First, ask yourself, "Why is it important to guard your heart?" I mean, it seems to me that the heart has a mind of its own. I guess that's why the saying goes, "The heart wants what it wants." However, just because it aches for something doesn't mean that what it desires is of good intent. If our goal is to be wise, then we must understand that the work we do to build ourselves is no causal thing. Our hearts hold a much greater purpose than what we have imagined. They are the source of how we think, feel, and act. Our hearts encompass who we are as a person. If you want to know your personality type, check your heart, because that is where your distinctive character is born.

We are instructed to guard our hearts because what we feel is experienced by the heart. All emotions experienced throughout our lifetime set the tone for our outlook on life. For example, when we feel lonely, our outlook on life can be "No one loves me, everyone has abandoned me, I am afraid to be alone." Our feelings can influence what we think and what we do. If we aren't careful, we can find ourselves in a cycle where life experiences confirm our negative beliefs. It is so easy to get lost in our choices that we eventually lose track of how things spiraled out of control in the first place.

We must take a step back and examine our hearts. We can learn to look at situations differently when we check our hearts. We cannot allow our emotions to control us but rather allow the presence of God to rule within us. Our hearts are the engine this body needs to function. The Bible speaks so forcefully about the state of our hearts because it is the driving force in making all decisions. Has your heart been guarded yet?

It is so important to understand the true intentions we all have. Healing our hearts takes time and work, but the Bible is the blueprint for how we should handle caring for such a fragile and sensitive matter. Read Proverbs 4:20-27. What are the key factors God points out to you to set you on the path of wisdom?

Day 3

A Purposed Heart

Good morning, beautiful.

Have you come across the viral image of a person grasping onto a rope, illustrating that holding on can cause more harm than good? Or perhaps the depiction of God holding a giant teddy bear behind His back, urging a little girl to let go of her tiny one? These images portray the idea that sometimes, we hold onto things that are important to us without realizing that something even more exceptional is waiting for us. Letting go can be difficult, especially when that item holds a lot of sentimental value, whether a person, place, or thing. But holding on results in us forfeiting our freedom.

The Bible says that God is a jealous God (Exodus 34:14), and He instructed us not to worship anything other than Him. That can include relationships, television, social media, work, friendships, and family. Whatever it may be, if it takes precedence over God, then it is considered an idol. God is calling us away from the idols in our lives because He no longer wants us to be perverted by their ideas.

Letting go requires you to have a purposed heart, one that is devoted to turning away from anything that may jeopardize your relationship with Christ. Can it be difficult? Yes! But wisdom is when you recognize the beauty of moving on and trusting the works of God in your life.

Sincerely,

Your friend

A Moment to Reflect

"But Daniel purposed in his heart that he would not defile himself with the portion of the king's meat, nor with the wine which he drank: therefore he requested of the prince of the eunuchs that he might not defile himself."

Daniel 1:8

I want you to pay attention to this line (v.8) where it says, "Daniel purposed in his heart." This means that Daniel decided that no matter the outcome, he was ready to give up his life to serve God. Daniel had the mindset, "If God's not in it, then I'm not with it!" He took a bold stand before some very high-ranked individuals to say that he would not damage his relationship with God to please man. He knew who he served, and because his faith and trust in God were strong, he didn't back down even when his life was potentially on the line.

To modernize Daniel's stance, it could equate to us continuing in a relationship knowing that it is not of God, choosing to return to something God has already taken you away from, or settling for what is because you lack faith in what is next. We all have been in this place before, and from one friend to another, I empathize with you. I understand that a void in your heart may be aching and seeking comfort. The way that you are trying to obtain it can also be the very thing irritating the wound rather than healing it.

It is important to know that when Daniel rejected the king's food, it had nothing to do with the consumption but rather what the food stood for. Here is a little history lesson: the food prepared for Daniel was forbidden by the law and not prepared according to Mosaic regulations[10] (see Leviticus 11). The meat is said to have been dedicated to idols.[11] So, in other words, Daniel did not want to partake in anything that could defile him in any way, but most importantly, sever his relationship with God.

If you are struggling to choose, remember this tidbit about Daniel. When he decided to reject the king's offer, Daniel was healthier and far better looking than the young men who ate the king's portions (see Daniel 1:15). That is the power of God when you can let go of what you think will save you to discover that it doesn't stand a chance against God. That is when you will begin seeing the shift in your life.

DAILY CHALLENGE

I love a good pros and cons list, so this morning, I want you to look hard at the idols in your life. What are the pros and cons of keeping things how they are? Then I want you to create another list and imagine what you can gain if you choose to change.

Day 4

Can You Follow Directions?

Good morning, beautiful.

In seventh grade, I had a teacher who gave us a quiz and told us to follow the directions. When finished, we were instructed to turn it over so she knew we were done. Being eager to have it completed, I neglected to read the directions thoroughly. It instructed me to "read everything carefully before doing anything." Let me emphasize "before doing anything." If I had read carefully, it would have saved me time and energy. If I had followed directions, I would have known that my only task was to write my name and put my pencil down.

Eagerness to finish was my downfall, and after I realized I had made a mistake, I felt embarrassed. I was focused on "what this teacher is going to think of me or what the other classmates will say knowing I was among the ones who didn't read correctly." Like that quiz, we are all in a test of our own called life. Each step comes with its own instructions. Right now, where you are, can you confidently say you know what has been asked of you?

This morning, our job is learning to listen and follow directions. The answer to your test is in your act of obedience. As Luke 11:28 says, "But he said, Yea rather, blessed are they that hear the word of God, and keep it." Our instructions are in God's Word! If you want answers, you now know where to go. Let's study God's Word so we can interpret His plans for us!

Sincerely,

Your friend

A Moment to Reflect

"Thou knowest the commandments, Do not commit adultery, Do not kill, Do not steal, Do not bear false witness, Defraud not, Honour thy father and mother. And he answered and said unto him, Master, all these have I observed from my youth. Then Jesus beholding him loved him, and said unto him, One thing thou lackest: go thy way, sell whatsoever thou hast, and give to the poor, and thou shalt have treasure in heaven: and come, take up the cross, and follow me."

Mark 10:19-21

We serve a God that knows our past, present, and future. From the time we entered our mother's womb, God says He knew us (see Jeremiah 1:5). So, I believe God will not instruct you to do something if it isn't associated with a plan and purpose. The issue is that we are not always privy to every step; therefore, we either don't follow the instructions or misinterpret the steps.

For example, the rich young ruler was a man who had great possessions, and he followed the commandments. Still, even in doing those things, when he encountered Jesus, he was looking for more. He wanted to know how to gain eternal life. Good news for him: Jesus had the answers! The sad news was that he had no idea what he had to lose to gain what he sought, so much so that when the answers were revealed to him, he walked away in sadness (see Mark 10:22). If you haven't already figured it out, the truth hurts, but that is God. He delivers the truth even when the information is uncomfortable to hear.

So, you may be asking, "What now?" You've made the necessary changes and worked so hard to build your relationship with Christ, which is fantastic. However, we are never complete until we depart from this earth. There is always room to grow; slowly but steadily, God is working on your heart to open it up to Him. If I haven't said it enough, then I want to repeat it: we are all here because we desire marriage, but the truth is, God used this adversity in your life to draw you closer to Him. Marriage will be a beautiful blessing, but what is it to gain the whole world and lose your soul? God knows what you want, but He is leading you in a way so you can receive but also manage the gift.

Being a follower of Christ is not easy, and there is a lot of giving before receiving. These moments do not occur out of hatefulness but out of love. God loves you so much that He doesn't want you to idolize the gift because it will one day fail you like every materialistic thing known to man. God cares more about your heart and, therefore, every direction He leads you in, that is the first and most important thing He aims to protect. God doesn't want us to lose sight of Him because, in man's failures, He knows that you will need something bigger and stronger to lift you up, so He operates so that you won't lose sight of Him even after He blesses you.

Instructions are important, so to save you time and energy, whether now or later, follow Christ because He knows what is best for you. One day, you will have more than the riches of this life; you will forever be God's eternal daughter, and that is the goal!

Daily Challenge

To be Christ's follower, we must learn how to reorder our priorities. Read Matthew 19:29. What is the Holy Spirit telling you today regarding your riches?

Day 5

Refiner

Good morning, beautiful.

Do you recall the assignment from your elementary school days when you had to create a masterpiece using clay? Kids were making bowls, mugs, plates, or whatever they could imagine, and we got to paint it, and then it went through the process of being hardened by heat. I remember some kids in my class didn't get to bring their artwork home because it exploded once heat was applied to it. Instructors gave us directions beforehand to ensure our art would survive this process. While some of us followed the instructions diligently, others didn't, and the outcomes of our choices were evident after the final test.

This memory reminds me of how we are God's masterpieces. Some of us can withstand the fire, and others are falling short and feeling beaten down by the wear and tear of this world. The Bible says that God is the potter, and we are the clay (see Isaiah 64:8). Everything that God does is a form of art, and at each step, He is refining us so we are ready for the fire.

Refine means "remove impurities or unwanted elements from a substance," according to the Oxford Dictionary. That means that God must remove unwanted elements and impurities that will jeopardize us. God is perfecting His work and plans to display you, but there is a process we must go through. Whether it be healing, renewing, sanctifying, releasing, or overcoming, this is your season to be worked on so you can live!

Sincerely,

Your friend

A Moment to Reflect

"I will bring the third part into the fire, and will refine them
as silver is refined, and will test them like gold is tested.
They will call on my name, and I will hear them. I will say,
'It is my people;' and they will say, 'the LORD is my God.'"

Zechariah 13:9

So, let's be honest: we all think about that beautiful diamond ring that will one day be placed on our hand, and we cannot wait for the day to finally say, "My husband!" We create Pinterest boards dedicated to the type of rings we want and the style of our wedding dresses because we are preparing for the future and changing our status from Ms. to Mrs.

In your pursuit of finding the perfect ring, have you ever stopped to research the process of making a diamond ring? Let me help you out—before a diamond is processed, it looks like a dull piece of glass. Then it is shipped off for cleaning. Afterwards, it goes into the process of being cut into the styles many people desire, such as princess, cushion, round, oval, and marquise. This process of cutting the diamond is a unique and skilled task. In fact, some describe it as an "extreme art."[12] Why? Because it takes specialized tools, knowledge, and technique. So, in other words, not just anybody can come in and cut a diamond. The process doesn't stop there; next, it must go through inspection and be graded, and once that is complete, it can be sold. That sounds like a lot of work, but I would say it is worth it, knowing the smiles it puts on people's faces when they see this beautiful display of art on their fingers, wrists, ears, and necks.

I bet you didn't know this, but diamonds are considered the hardest material known to man, so much so that to cut a diamond, another diamond must be used to cut it. Sounds familiar? It's almost like that saying, "Iron sharpens iron." That said, the Bible tells us that we go through a process of being refined. Not just anything can come and prune us and shape us. Nor can anything come in and determine our value. It takes something that is of the same caliber as us to make the necessary changes we need. If you haven't guessed already, I am referring to God.

We were all made in His image (Genesis 1:27); therefore, only through God can we achieve the identity we were destined to have since the beginning of time. The tests and trials we endure in this life are part of a process that supersedes our understanding. However, I can share with you that when we are tested, we have been refined, and we soon enter the next step of determining our value.

You may not feel it yet, but from experience, it's an honor to be pruned. I promise you that the transformation will be worth it in the end. By staying in the race, you can go from dull to dazzling. In this season, God is adding value to your life.

DAILY CHALLENGE

Take a moment to read Leviticus 26:12-13 and consider what God is conveying to you. How is He reminding you of the ways He is currently fighting for you, or recalling moments in your life when He was present?

Week 5

Build My Life

The one thing that I hate the most is feeling as though I am stuck in a box. I am someone who enjoys walking to the rhythm of my own beat. I never would describe myself as a follower . I prefer to challenge the status quo because I believe that to change, one must be open to doing something different. It was easy for me to challenge others' thinking, but I found it hard when I had to be in a place to challenge myself. Even when others challenged me, I didn't respond well to being told my way wasn't the only way. My mom always told me, "You can't be so heavenly bound that you are no earthly good." I had difficulty knowing how to balance my relationship with God and still be human.

I am someone who values a deep connection. In my pursuit of knowing God, I held on tightly to His Word because that was the only thing I could trust. God put me in a place where He challenged me and opened my heart to trust His Word and the experiences He would send me through. One way God began to open my eyes was when He led me to read a book called *Dangerous Prayer,* by Craig Groeshel. The book referenced Psalm 139:23-24 which says, "Search me, O God, and know my heart: try me, and know my thoughts: And see if there be any wicked way in me, and lead me in the way everlasting." Something about this scripture pierced my heart, and I began to have a more profound desire for God to lead me into unmarked territory. I felt challenged to not hold on to God's Word out of fear but out of trust, knowing that if God brought me to it, He would get me through it.

When we ask God to deepen our relationship with Him, it may lead us to the truth that we don't want to hear, but it is necessary for our growth. God had to show me the only way to freedom is through Him. Therefore, to trust in Him, I had to surrender my understanding. God led me in a way that challenged my thoughts and put me in a position where I had to truly ponder if there was enough evidence to prove my way of thinking was correct. I am secure enough to say that my thought process about life was grim, and if I hadn't allowed God to correct it, it would have soiled the future that God had for me.

Saying those dangerous prayers put me in a position for God to build my life on His love. I endured a lot, but God helped me find my voice and allowed things to shift so I could see the steadiness of His foundation. God led me to take different approaches to living life; He allowed me to stand on the principles of His Word and not to allow the chaos of this world to steer me off course. He allowed me to see that I could face rejection and survive. I was open to seeing that I could make a different choice. He showed me I was enough, and the difference between spiritual and physical waiting. He removed the barriers from the box I had unknowingly put myself in. I now had larger parameters to walk in because God reclaimed the territory that the enemy tried to steal from me.

There are so many levels to get through while on the path God has carved out, and there are days when it seems impossible. However, as my reader, I want you to know that this is your season of being refined. God is building your life, and like every building, it takes a solid foundation to grant permission to start building the next level. I challenge you this week to say the prayers that invite the test into our lives. Yes, I said it: ask the test into our lives because it is time that we prove to ourselves that we are capable and strong enough to withstand the trials that may come our way. God is granting you access, and you have been approved!

Day 1

Faith is the Only Requirement

Good morning, beautiful.

How do you respond when you feel God is silent in your life? I would immediately assume I had done something wrong and feel guilt, shame, and hopelessness. All these thoughts and feelings would swirl through my mind, and I would find myself many nights crying to sleep because I thought God was done with me.

If I had wallowed in self-pity, the enemy would have had me thinking that God had left me and that there was no point in return. Luckily, I somehow drew closer to God by crying my eyes out. I realized that it wasn't just God holding my hand but that I was holding His hand back. Just as He would reach out and grab me, God had shown me more times than I could count that I always had access to Him.

Faith kept me going, and I have learned that faith will align you with Christ. In Christ, you cannot have faith without hope and hope without faith. Faith is the only requirement to being made whole. God is steadily filling your foundation, and He is adding levels. To achieve the finished product, we must hold on to the faith God gave us when we first started praying. If you are struggling to hear God this season, know He hasn't let go of your hand, but this is the season where you reach out and squeeze tighter than ever. This time, you hold God's hand and don't let go.

Sincerely,

Your friend

A Moment to Reflect

*"And Jesus said, Somebody hath touched me:
for I perceive that virtue is gone out of me."*

Luke 8:46

People come to God for various reasons. Some come because they want to be healed, escape their situations, be free from sin, and many other things. You hear people thanking God and praising Him all the time. Through those thanks, God hears and sees us all. So much so that some people may shy away from Jesus because they feel their little voices won't be heard or they think God won't see them because they are nobody. In the book of Luke, we learn of one woman who, in a crowded, noisy place, cultivated Jesus's attention. He stopped in His tracks and asked, "Who touched me?" (v. 45). This person's name is unknown, but her problem was that she struggled with the issue of blood.

Jesus knew something was different about her touch because He felt His power leave Him. So, imagine how this went down. Here, a crowd of people surrounded Jesus, calling His name and touching whatever they could get to. In the sea of hands and voices, Jesus continued to walk through the crowd unchanged. How does this translate in today's day and time? Well, for starters, God says in His Word, "Not every one that saith unto me, Lord, Lord, shall enter into the kingdom of heaven; but he that doeth the will of my Father which is in heaven" (Matthew 7:21). There are many who will say the name Jesus but do not possess the power that comes with calling His name. The Will that scripture speaks of is no other than Christ Himself. The secret is faith and knowing what God has done for us at the Cross.

Many people will shout Jesus's name, but only a few will advance in the Kingdom of God. The woman with the issue of blood wasn't coming for Jesus to get what she could. She wasn't coming to Him so she could boast about her encounter. Instead, she came to Him because she was tired from trying everything else. She was tired of this world failing her and leaving her with nothing but unanswered questions. She was tired of accepting defeat. She came to Jesus because she had the mindset that she was going to give it her all and she was going to see about a Man that she had heard healed people. She found herself in that crowd by word of mouth and pressed her way through because her faith encouraged her to keep fighting. She didn't care about touching His hand or grabbing His leg. She wanted to connect and hoped it was enough to receive her healing.

The woman with the issue of blood provides us with one of the most incredible demonstrations of humbleness. Instead of waiting for God to touch her, she demonstrated that all we must do is raise our hands out and touch God to receive what we need. He has given us access to where we can go to Him in our times of trouble. It takes faith and courage to get to that place, but when you have faith and press your way through the sea of noise, God will meet you because when you have an encounter with Him a change must take place, just as the woman with the issue of blood received her healing; she went from being sick to healed.

DAILY CHALLENGE

What does it mean to touch the hem of God's garment? How is God speaking to you on this matter regarding your needs? I will encourage you to pray this morning, but I want you to do it a little differently. This time in your praying, instead of asking God to come to you, I want you to lay it all out in the open. Begin to reveal and lay your burdens at God's feet.

Day 2

Everything That Glitters Isn't Gold

Good morning, beautiful.

Have you ever heard of "Trauma Bonds"? These occur when an abuser manipulates a victim, often someone who has experienced emotional or relational trauma in the past, causing the victim to become reliant on the abuser for validation and care. When we fail to address past traumas, we become more susceptible to developing future relationships based on trauma.

What should be viewed as a threat or danger can be mistakenly perceived as a place of comfort. Red flags are mistaken for green ones, and what appears shiny and shimmering turns out to be dull and dim. There is a reason why the Bible tells us to know them by the fruit they bear (Matthew 7:15-20). What is the fruit? Love, joy, peace, longsuffering, gentleness, goodness, faith, meekness, and temperance (Galatians 5: 22-23). However, the same can be said about us. If we are not walking in the fruit, how can we recognize those same qualities in someone else?

God takes time to shape our lives, and in those moments of intimacy with Him, our true selves are revealed. However, we must first be willing to be vulnerable and open ourselves up to Him. God desires to rid us of things that lead us to dark places and instead bring us back to life, revitalizing and refreshing us. Through this, we can bear good fruit and become recognizable by it.

Sincerely,

Your friend

A Moment to Reflect

"And when he saw a fig tree in the way, he came to it, and found nothing thereon, but leaves only, and said unto it, Let no fruit grow on thee henceforward forever. And presently, the fig tree withered away."

Matthew 21:19

Have you ever endured a moment where the idea of something was far better than the reality of it? For example, have you ever tried a new food and the presentation of what sits in front of you is alluring, but within that first bite, you realize that the taste of this food is not delicious? So naturally, what happens next? You will probably be disappointed and dissatisfied, right? Matthew 21:17-22 speaks on the parable of the barren fig tree. Jesus approached the tree because He was looking for food. With His knowledge, He knew that this tree should have borne fruit, so He went forward only to find that it was empty and did not yield what it was made to produce.

At first glance, when reading verse 19, you don't quite understand why God would want to curse the tree. I promise it wasn't because it didn't have food. The curse is because the tree presented to be something that it was not, meaning it was "fake." Have you ever endured a moment like this where someone appeared to be something they weren't, especially during a time when you really needed what they were offering? This is upsetting, and honestly, it can cause many of us to stumble and fall because we were desperately searching and hoping to find what we needed. Like us, Jesus was upset at this tree because it did not live up to its purpose.

Jesus was searching for a way to be fed. Though this was a physical sensation He experienced, it is similar to what we experience as Christians. How many of you are struggling internally with a desire to be fed? How many of you have tried to fill your voids with people, places, or things? Are you tired of coming up short? Or shall I say, are you tired of being disappointed that these things can never satisfy your needs? So many people on this earth are masked and appear fruitful. Still, once you get past their presentation, you realize that all they offered was a pretty appearance, nothing of substance.

When you are in a place of hunger like Jesus was, it is easy to be fooled because you are more susceptible to manipulation. Being in a constant place of hurt and seeking validation leads us to confusion and uncertainty. God does not want you to hunger for the wrong things that will lead you to be disappointed. God wants to show you how to recognize what is real fruit and what is disguised as fruit. God cursed the tree because He made it a point that no one should have to endure what He experienced. God knows that you are searching, and as you come to Him, He wants to set the standard of what it means to be authentic. God wants to be the actual depiction of "Ask, and it shall be given you; seek, and ye shall find; knock, and it shall be opened unto you" (Matthew 7:7). God doesn't want you to leave empty-handed!

DAILY CHALLENGE

To recognize the fruit of the spirit in others, you must first recognize it within yourself. How do you feel your life reflects the fruit of the spirit?

Day 3

Surrender in the Chaos

Good morning, beautiful.

Life has a funny way of knowing how to beat us down. Some may struggle with stressors from their jobs, family, health problems, or relational troubles. All these things can cause us to feel rocky and unsettled in our environment. Ultimately, they can cause our foundation to be less sturdy. The word of God says, "Come unto me all ye that labor and are heavy laden, and I will give you rest" (Matthew 11:28), meaning those who feel worn down and overwhelmed. God, however, has the answer, and He tells us that if you are feeling submerged by life's pressures, rest in Him.

To take a rest means to be still and drown out the noise. We must understand that we are not exempt from troubles because we call ourselves Christians. However, as Christians, we know that there is shelter under the mighty wings of God. We can either choose to panic or choose to be at peace with life's difficulties. Sound decisions are never made from a frantic mindset, but rather when we take the time to lay our burdens before Jesus.

This is the time that we choose surrender over chaos. We may not be able to control the storms we face, but we can control how we respond. God doesn't want you to tire from fighting these battles.

The best place to be is at the feet of Jesus. There, your strength will be renewed, and you will find healing. So I tell you, "Come ALL." It's time to find that place of rest so God can make you whole again.

Sincerely,

Your friend

A Moment to Reflect

"And they feared exceedingly, and said one to another,
What manner of man is this, that even the wind and the sea obey
him?"

Mark 4:41

I often think about how amazing the disciples had it! They got to walk with Jesus and witness the miracles He performed with their own eyes. They had front-row seats to see God's power, so I find it funny that they would be intimidated by a storm. At this point in their ministry, one would assume that they should have had enough faith to be asleep like Jesus instead of being frightened. They should have believed that this storm would pass without causing harm to anyone. But let me ask you this question: how many times have you seen God show up in your life, and yet the minute challenges come your way; you are struck with fear? It happens to the best of us, just as it did the disciples.

As you read through the Bible, you will soon learn that there are two types of fear. One type is encouraged in all believers, and that is to fear God. In contrast, the other type of fear is known as the spirit of fear (see 2 Timothy 1:7). If you were to look up the definition of fear, it states, "an unpleasant emotion caused by the belief that someone or something is dangerous, likely to cause pain or threat." Mark chapter 4 describes both types of fears the disciples encountered on their journey. One is that they feared the storm because it threatened their safety. They probably assumed that they would not make it to their destination, or worse, they could all have been severely injured. This is probably why they came to Jesus and woke Him up, saying, "Master, carest thou not that we perish?" (Mark 4: 38). They were afraid, and rightly so; there was a big storm that they were worried about. However, they missed the most important clue Jesus provided them before entering the storm. He said, "Let us pass over unto the other side" (Mark 4: 35). With Jesus being the Son of God, and we being the children of God, we cannot perish, because Jesus cannot perish. Jesus, at that time, reassured them that they were indeed going to make it to the other side. Jesus didn't tell them all of the details about their journey.

Through that opposition in their lives, the Disciples encountered the reality of spiritual fear, but they also were a witness to the God-giving fear that Jesus had been talking to them about. They learned that God was greater than the storm. They learned the true power of Christ and that through Him, they would have nothing to fear because God can overcome it all! If God said you are healed, then you are healed. If God said you are delivered, then you are delivered. If God said you will one day be married, then you will one day be married. God sometimes omits the details in His plan, but just as He gave the disciples clarity before entering the storm, God is giving you peace in knowing that you will make it to the other side if He is in the boat with you. Don't allow the winds and waves to cause you to be frantic; instead, surrender to God in the chaos and follow His lead.

DAILY CHALLENGE

Read Psalms 31. Storms are going to come our way, and we can either choose Christ or choose chaos. God's Word is your most powerful weapon, so the best way to fight this fight is to know the truth about what is to come. What is God saying to you this morning through this scripture?

Day 4

Redeemed

Good morning, beautiful.

Recently, I had to bury a loved one, and death is never easy. Whenever I have dealt with death, it makes me think about the meaning of life. I've attended some funerals for family members and felt numb because I never had the opportunity to develop a relationship with them. It was never because I didn't want to, but because their strongholds kept us apart. I have also attended funerals of people who weren't blood related. Still, their loss was more impactful because they stepped in and filled a role out of love and compassion toward me.

I sometimes imagine the moment when we are absent from the body and no longer fighting the spiritual battles of this world. If allowed to glimpse what we could have been, would we be disappointed, knowing we had the power to overcome but chose to be bound, or would we be pleased with what we overcame and our impact on others?

I know I am getting deep, but I am learning that we get one life, and when it's done, it's done. Living your life is not all about partying and experiencing what life offers. Living your life is truly a responsibility. Evil is all around us, and our time should be spent redeeming what is ours and not forfeiting our time for worthless things.

Sincerely,

Your friend

A Moment to Reflect

"See then that ye walk circumspectly, not as fools, but as wise, Redeeming the time, because the days are evil."

Ephesians 5:15-16

How do you define time? Or better yet, what are you prioritizing? I ask these questions because we get 24 hours a day, seven days a week, and if you had to take a snapshot of what that week consisted of, how many hours of the day are you actually productive? I don't mean the time you spend at work, school, or home, but how productive are you when it comes to incorporating God's plan into your everyday activities?

Examples of how this could look would be making time to pray, studying His Word, volunteering at the church, inviting someone to church, sharing your testimony, and manifesting the fruit of the spirit in your everyday encounters with people. One area that has proven to be both crucial and fulfilling is starting your day with the right decisions to honor God. Scripture reminds us that the days are evil, and it's easy to be led astray. Knowing our Heavenly Father is essential to avoid distractions and negative influences. As we draw closer to Him, we become more attuned to His plans for us, gaining clarity and discernment.

Redeeming your time is when you no longer allow anyone or anything to interrupt what God is doing in your life. This is your season to regain the seconds, minutes, and hours the enemy tried to steal from you when he had you in bondage. It is time to take full advantage of God, because what He has in store for you is a one-time deal. We must jump on the opportunity of knowing Him because, I am telling you, time is precious. There are no do-overs once we leave this earth.

DAILY CHALLENGE

How can you make this time in your life impactful for the building up of God's kingdom? The kingdom isn't the four walls of the church building, but the people God has called you to serve. You don't need big titles to have a purpose; you just need God, who will care for everything else.

Day 5

Take up Your Position

Good morning, beautiful.

Have you ever had a moment when you knew you needed to do something, but for whatever reason, it felt like you could not get to it? Then suddenly, when you finally get a chance to cross that one thing off your to-do list, BOOM, the answer to your prayers is right in front of you. It's as if God delayed you so you could arrive on time.

I promise it really is something magical when you have that on-time moment. It's that little reminder that God cares for you and loves you. I am reminded of Deuteronomy 31:8, which says "God will never leave nor forsake you." Do you know what forsake means? It means to abandon. So, God is saying that He is not going to leave us. He will not cease to support, condemn us, give up on us, or discontinue before completion. Lastly, He will not allow us to fail or leave us to our own despair.

So, as we end this week, I want you to anticipate God being an on-time God. You must be the one to trust in Him and know that God will not bring you to something without having a way through it. Life is a series of tests, but the right test will teach us a lesson and open our hearts to invite God in. Remember, God does not go against our will, but if you open yourself up to it, I promise you will see the promise!

Sincerely,

Your friend

A Moment to Reflect

"Then said he unto me, Fear not, Daniel: for from the first day that thou didst set thine heart to understand, and to chasten thyself before thy God, thy words were heard, and I am come for thy words."

Daniel 10:12

"Fear not" is what this scripture begins with. I feel that it speaks of the power of God, because there is nothing on this earth we should be afraid of. Not only does this scripture remind us not to fear, but I also feel it validates a lot of what we think and do when it comes to waiting on God. The angel spoke to Daniel and eased his mind by letting him know that we were never forgotten from the moment we started to pray. God had our answers ready, and they're on the way to being delivered. Daniel had patience and remained in the right position to hear from God.

That position was at the feet of Jesus. Take Martha and Mary, for example. Martha was busy running around trying to cook and clean, but Mary sat at Jesus's feet to hear the Word (see Luke 10:38-42). Jesus had to educate Martha to let her know that those other things are unimportant, but what really matters is the Word He was sharing with her that will help her when He is no longer there. Don't get swept up by all your to-do's. I am sure Daniel had many things he felt he needed to do at that time, but he made God a priority, he prayed, and he fasted until he heard from God.

We may not be able to physically see the spiritual warfare that is before us, but God sees it all. Your delayed answer may be because God is fighting for you and clearing the path so your answer can arrive. Understand that silence does not equate to no. The enemy wants you to feel defeated; he knows how valuable time is on this earth. So, trust and believe he will ambush the answers God has for you with all his strength because, for him, a delay is an opportunity to get you to turn your back on God.

Just remember that time and patience are key to winning in this race. It is so important that you don't give up until you have received your answer from God! While you are waiting, use this time to grow within yourself. You must get to a place where you are confident in who God is raising you up to be. This is the time when you exercise your power of control. You can't control when and where the answer will arrive, but you can control your position until it does. Will you be seated before Jesus or turned away because you grew impatient and valued your time over God?

Daily Challenge

God will respond whether the answer is yes or no, so this morning, I want you to create a memory list. Write down all the things you have brought to God's attention, and as He answers them, check them off your list. Keep this as a reminder that God does indeed hear you!

Week 6

If it's Hysterical, it's Historical.

When I was growing up, I would have some outrageous temper tantrums. I can recall when I stomped up the stairs, slammed doors, and talked back to my mom. At those moments, I would feel so unregulated and fed up that I would explode. It was hard to articulate my feelings because I felt everything at once. I struggled greatly with thinking I was misunderstood because I felt no one respected my boundaries. I felt I always had to make room for others, but no one would ever make room for me. Fast forward to my adolescent/teenage years. I found myself having very relaxed boundaries and not being confident enough to know I was enough. All these things made me very angry, but instead of expressing it, I held it in. I allowed so many negative feelings and thoughts to shape my perspective of life.

It wasn't until I was much older that I heard the saying, "If it's hysterical, it's historical," meaning that if a situation causes an out-of-proportion response, it is likely because your trigger is based on something you have endured. It was hard to understand that concept because my reactions to triggers were never outward expressions. Instead, I held everything within, struggled with negative thinking, and had poor attachments to people. I found myself disassociating and not knowing how to be present. I learned that when I turned inward and drew away from others, I realized that my silence was my response to stressful situations. That's when I learned that I was indeed triggered, and some internal work needed to be done so I could heal.

My younger self always dreamed of finding "the one" and getting married because I felt that being married would solve my problems. I thought it would give me the freedom I had always desired but couldn't obtain alone. The thought, "I make room for others, but no one makes room for me," led me to settle and think that if I loved hard enough, that would be enough. God showed me the strength of my heart: I am a giver, kind, and compassionate. However, He also revealed my weak spots in that I was distant, avoidant, in pain, and not receptive. Because of my negative thoughts, I couldn't see the love always standing right before me. I had allowed my negative beliefs to become my truth, and misery and anxiety followed.

God showed me that my singleness wasn't a trial but that it was the process I needed to open my heart so that I could receive not just the blessing of marriage but that I could receive the love and comfort my Father in Heaven had for me. All the pre-work of enduring breakups, losing friends, depression, and struggling with confidence served a much greater purpose than I had realized then. God wanted my heart, and what I had seen as damaged and no good, God saw as a piece of art. So, towards the end of 2021, God told me that my word for 2022 was healing. All I could say was, "Jesus, take the wheel." Of course, I questioned, because I had no idea what God meant. Through prayer, God revealed that in 2022, I would learn that I could change. My negative beliefs would no longer serve a purpose, because this time I would see that I am enough and that there is room for me.

Not knowing the whole totality of God's plan, I entered 2022 with the determination to find healthier coping skills to deal with my anxiety. I decided to inquire about therapy for myself. My therapist was the best; she helped me see the root of my negative beliefs that stemmed from my childhood. She told me one little thing that began the jumpstart of my healing. She said, "It's just a difference in preferences." What she was saying is that what I considered forbidden gestures was nothing more than a difference in preferences. That simple explanation unlocked my mind and made me realize that I have choices. I had to understand that no one was perfect, and through that realization, I allowed my inner child to heal.

This week, I invite you into a place of healing and becoming present with your wounds, so you no longer see them as damage but rather the opportunity that makes us unique to our purpose here on this earth. I want to leave you with this promise, "So shall my word be that goeth forth out of my mouth: it shall not return unto me void, but it shall accomplish that which I please, and it shall prosper in the thing whereto I sent it" (Isaiah 55:11). This chapter of your life will have its ups and downs, but rest assured that God will not leave His work unfinished. Everything you endure serves a purpose, so trust that His promises will be fulfilled in due time.

Day 1

This is my MOTTO

Good morning, beautiful.

What are typical sayings you grew up with in your household? I have a few examples to jog your memory: "What happens in this house stays in this house," "If it ain't broke, don't fix it," and "Fake it till you make it!" Are you having a nostalgia moment yet? These sayings, or shall I say "mottoes," are what most of us grew up with. Mottoes are beliefs that guide you; they represent one's values and stance on life. I must say, though, not all mottoes are good ones to follow. Have you ever asked yourself, "Where did they derive from?" It is human nature to gravitate to things that are pleasing to the flesh. If it sounds good, then it must be good, right? It is so easy to get caught up in the whirlwind of trends when we don't understand the origin or message of the things we speak.

A big component of healing is re-examining the totality of your life. A thought is never just a thought because, nine times out of ten, it was the product of something planted in your mind. Day in and day out, God is sowing good seeds into your fertilized ground, but the enemy is lurking behind Him and planting seeds of his own (see Matthew 13: 24-43). Therefore, knowing where you are receiving your information from is important. As the saying goes, "Life is what you make it," but are your beliefs rooted in the fertilized ground, or has the enemy been choking out the truth with his weeds?

Sincerely,

Your friend

A Moment to Reflect

"A man's belly shall be satisfied with the fruit of his mouth;
and with the increase of his lips shall he be filled.
Death and life are in the power of the tongue:
and they that love it shall eat the fruit thereof."

Proverbs 18:20-21

Many of us have heard the phrase "Do as I say and not as I do" from our parents. It's a complex saying, because it's easy to talk the talk, but can we walk the walk when our actions don't match our words? Some say that this means, "I don't want you to make the same mistakes I did," or "I want you to do better than I did." While these are admirable goals, the Bible teaches us that faith without works is dead (see James 2:14-26). So why do we settle for words without actions?

The book of Proverbs emphasizes the value of wisdom. What we believe often translates into the words we utter, and if they stem from negativity, we may end up speaking evil over our own lives. Not all sayings are inherently wrong, but the devil can deceive us by twisting their underlying meanings. For instance, the phrase "What happens in this house stays in this house" may seem harmless, but it can be detrimental in certain situations. What if your family was abusive, and you needed to seek help? Or what if you need advice on how to cope with stressors? The saying can prevent us from receiving the help we need. It is crucial to be mindful of our words and their implications.

In essence, our words have power, and they can either build us up or tear us down. This is why it is crucial to be mindful of what we say and to whom we speak. We must use our words to uplift others and ourselves, rather than to cause harm or division. As the book of Proverbs says, "The tongue has the power of life and death, and those who love it will eat its fruit" (Proverbs 18:21 NIV). Therefore, we must speak life over ourselves and others, even when it may seem difficult to do so. With this mindset, we can create a positive environment that promotes growth, healing, and unity.

It's important to recognize that healing isn't always easy, and it often takes time. However, a willingness to let go of past hurts and embrace new perspectives can go a long way in promoting healing. This requires a certain level of self-awareness and a willingness to confront and challenge one's own beliefs and behaviors. It's a process that requires patience, compassion, and a commitment to growth. Ultimately, though, the reward of newfound peace and freedom is well worth the effort. So take a deep breath, trust the journey, and know that healing is possible.

Daily Challenge

Let's fact check! Today, let's put your mottoes to the test. Do they truly represent your core values and uplift your life, or do they leave you feeling empty and lost? Let's find out.

Day 2

When the Dust Settles

Good morning, beautiful.

Not too long ago, I was cleaning my kitchen and accidentally broke one of my glass cups. I carefully ensured I picked up all the glass pieces and placed everything in the trash. A few days passed, and I realized my trash can was full, so I took the garbage out. Lo and behold, as I picked up the trash bag, I somehow cut myself. I immediately went into shock because all I saw was blood spewing from my hand. My brain's alarm system sounded off, and I was no longer thinking from a place of logic but rather a place of panic. After my anxiety died down and I stopped the bleeding, I was sitting on my bed and instantly remembered the broken glass pieces that lay at the bottom of the trash bag.

After the dust settled, I had time to ponder what had happened. I wondered how often we have moments when we think we have handled a problem in our lives and believe it is over, but it comes back to cut us. One lesson I have learned in the aftermath of life's problems is that it is better to be proactive and not reactive—learning what to do or not to do before disaster comes.

I could have let that incident wreck my day, but instead, I chose joy and appreciated the fact that I was okay and that my wound would heal with time. Understand that there will be trouble in this life, but it won't last too long with the right teacher to lead the way.

Sincerely,

Your friend

A Moment to Reflect

"And one of them smote the servant of the high priest, and cut off his right ear. And Jesus answered and said, Suffer ye thus far. And he touched his ear, and healed him."

Luke 22:50-51

What do you think Jesus meant when He said, "Suffer ye thus far?" It sounds like a plea, as if He is begging someone not to overreact to what has just occurred. As you see in Luke 22:50, someone has just attacked the high priest's servant because they had come to detain Jesus. The individual who smote the servant was no other than Peter, the impulsive but dedicated follower of Christ. Just by the looks of it, it appeared Peter was thinking from his feeling brain (fight, flight, freeze responses) rather than his thinking brain (understanding right from wrong).

Peter responded from a place of love, not wanting the Roman soldiers to harm Jesus. He did not realize that moment was all part of God's plan. During Jesus' ministry, He had prepared the disciples for what was to come. Of course, like any human being, we listen, but we also have our own ideology for what we think will happen. Sometimes, we can put aside the things that are too painful to focus on because our hearts and brains are not ready to accept the reality of it all. You may be experiencing trouble in your life, and maybe to cope with it, you have turned to destructive avenues in your attempt to escape. If this is you, I would like you to sit momentarily with the feelings coming up. Take time to be present and not rush from what you are experiencing. I want you to know that it is going to be okay!

Peter acted destructively, and he could have easily derailed and felt defeated. However, his great Teacher gave him the tools to correct his wrongs. When Peter attacked the servant, it wasn't about what happened at the moment that taught the lesson, but how Peter recovered and continued on the path God had laid out before him.

How you move on from stressful events reveals the truth in what you have learned from spending time with God. Old wounds can open back up, but God didn't orchestrate this to trouble you. Rather, He picked the circumstances to reveal that you can handle what you thought would kill you. Or better yet, He reveals that you can handle what you thought was too much or too painful. God is revealing the inner strength that is within you. Time spent with God is time well spent. He is teaching you ways to cope and be at peace in His presence.

Today, let's place one hand on our chests and the other on our bellies, and together, we take one slow breath in and another long breath out. Instead of fighting chaos, we choose peace. We choose to think from a place of logic and reason rather than be distraught and panicked. God knows the sensitivity of your needs, so don't delay this time to know Him more.

DAILY CHALLENGE

We all make mistakes in how we handle life's stressors. So don't fret, because now that we have experienced what not to do let's learn how to better manage our stressors.

Reflect on a personal situation that has caused you stress in your life.

Now that you have identified a situation, ask yourself the following questions:

a. What feelings (sad, angry, disappointed, etc.) did you have at that moment?
b. What was your response (action) when dealing with the situation?
c. How would you rate the helpfulness of the response on a scale from 1 (not helpful) to 10 (very helpful)? If it wasn't helpful, what are three alternative options you could have pursued to solve the issue?

The more you know about yourself and your triggers, the better you can explore healthy coping mechanisms to deal with stressors when they arrive.

Day 3

I Can Benefit from
What's not Visible to Me

Good morning, beautiful.

Right now I am on this kick of trying to lose weight and be healthy. I have tried and failed several times because I quit prematurely when I didn't see the results when I wanted to see them. It is unfortunate not to be born with the gift of seeing a change in real-time. The con of not having this feature is that we don't see the small shifts that happen. We have little to no evidence to support our decision to change.

I can tell you that trying to change is hard, but so is choosing to stay the same. Before deciding to do something different, we must believe that change is possible. For example, we know people can lose weight, so if I say I can, I must have confidence that it can be done. True confidence can never be experienced without elements of faith. I hope by now you have it nailed and stapled in your heart. Hebrews 11:1, "Now faith is the substance of things hoped for and the evidence of things not seen."

We will never see life as God sees it, which is hard to accept. However, the beauty in trusting God lies in knowing you will receive more than you requested. Change is taking place, and even though you may not see all that is happening, have confidence in the good choices you are making today. This journey towards healing doesn't happen in real-time, but at the right time, you will reap the benefits and the reward for not giving up!

Sincerely,

Your friend

A Moment to Reflect

"Then enquired he of them the hour when he began to amend. And they said unto him, Yesterday at the seventh hour the fever left him."

John 4:52

I know I talk a lot about faith, but trust me when I tell you that faith can get you to many places and open many doors. The trick is that you must believe in what you can't see. For many people, we like tangible things. We prefer to utilize our senses (taste, smell, touch, sight, and hearing) to tell us that what we are experiencing is real. However, our natural gifts can also be our downfall when we depend too heavily on ourselves. We won't always see what God is doing in real-time, making it hard to wait for change. However, by building your faith muscle, you will soon know that mountains will move when commanded by God.

Today's scripture tells the story of one man's quest to heal his son. He was a nobleman from Capernaum who needed a miracle for his son. He heard that Jesus was in Galilee, and faith led him to seek healing for his child. Now, I can almost imagine that this nobleman had a lot of ideas running through his brain of just how Jesus would heal his son. Maybe he thought Jesus would follow him back to Capernaum because that seemed the most logical way to complete this task. I imagine the nobleman assuming healing would only come if Jesus touched his son. So when Jesus threw this nobleman a whammy and said, "Go your way; your son lives" (John 4:50 NKJV). I can almost imagine the gut-wrenching feeling he had because there was no tangible evidence that the task was done.

If you all think we have it bad now, back then there weren't any cell phones to call house members to confirm the healing. This nobleman's faith was being tested. He had to choose whether to keep walking in faith or wallow in defeat. It is hard to hope for what is when the right now seems dreadful. I love this story of the nobleman because he didn't know what to expect, but he chose to have faith anyhow. He relied on what he had heard about Jesus and believed healing would be bestowed upon his home and family. Through his faith, he experienced more than what he had bargained for. He realized that not just the hands of God heal, but His Words also carry power.

We may not always know how God will heal, but we know He is a Healer. We may not always know when the healing will happen, but we know God is a Man of His Word. Don't allow your eyes to make you miss what God is doing in your life. If God promised you that you would be healed and set free from the things that have kept you captive, then all you must do is believe. Like the man in this story, you can also experience the healing you long for. Keep moving forward, and don't give up.

Daily Challenge

Take a moment to reflect on the changes you have experienced through God.

1. How have those changes bettered your life?
2. How are you different?
3. What stops you from holding on to faith for the prayers that haven't been answered yet?
4. What are the pros and cons of moving forward or giving up?

Day 4

Wrongfully Accused

Good morning, beautiful.

Since the beginning of humankind, blame has been an element interwoven into our genetic makeup. This stems from Adam and Eve in the garden (see Genesis 3:1-7). Eve ate the forbidden fruit, and her husband Adam also partook and ate the fruit. When Jesus confronted them about it, they both blamed everything and everyone but themselves. What do you think happens when there isn't anything or anyone to assign blame to?

We can teach all day long that every life decision has a cause and an effect, but what if what's happening in your life didn't result from something you did wrong? What if your current situation has no assigned blame? Who takes accountability for something that you had no control over? Life can have more questions than answers, and that alone can cause stress and feelings of defeat.

God provides us with great examples of His power and glory. Take, for instance, the woman with the issue of blood. I wonder how she felt, having an infirmity she did not choose. I wonder how Esther felt when called to a position she did not choose. I wonder what you think about struggling with life's challenges that you did not choose. We may not know why or what led us to where we are now, but we do know that through Jesus, our lives can be changed. Maybe there isn't anyone to blame because God wants the glory for what will happen in your life. He wants others to see that He holds power and reigns victorious.

Sincerely,

Your friend

A MOMENT TO REFLECT

*"And his disciples asked him, saying, Master, who did sin, this man,
or his parents, that he was born blind? Jesus answered,
Neither hath this man sinned, nor his parents:
but that the works of God should be made manifest in him."*

John 9:2-3

Don't you hate it when something goes wrong and the first thing people ask is, "What did you do?" I am starting to believe that the reason we love to place the blame on someone is that it gives us a way out. No one must think extra hard or be open to anything different. Assigning blame is all the evidence one needs to prove their theory is correct, even if it is wrong.

Being wrongly accused can lead to feelings of anger and annoyance. It can make you guarded and defensive. It is generally hard to trust at this point, and we can experience resentment. This can create a wall between us and those surrounding us, and we withdraw and feel lonely. On the outside looking in, blame may not seem all that bad, but it can cause damage to one's mental and emotional health. Let me ask you this. How does it feel for you to assign blame versus being blamed?

In today's scripture, we see a question being asked by the disciples, and they are inquiring if this man's disability was the result of a person's sin. If the disciples questioned this issue, I wonder how many others before them assumed that this man's afflictions resulted from his doings or that of his family. Many people don't realize that we are all sinners because of man's rebellion against God. We live in a fallen world; therefore, there will be tribulations (see John 16:13).

Some of us have visible disabilities while others may be less detectable, but it doesn't make one better. If we were all perfect, then none of us would need God. In John 9:1-3 we learn that the blind man's position in life wasn't because he did something wrong or that his parents made a mistake, but rather to simply show the power of God at work. God's purpose was to show that men were free by His power and His power alone. Not only that, but God's gospel was spread through one man's healing, and it provided an invitation to know who God is and what He can do.

Your season and current situations allow God to reveal Himself and His plan. I don't care what your friends or family have said about you. God wants to do work in your life, and He uses this adversity to reveal Himself. Take your eyes off the situation and place them back on God. Remember that everything is orchestrated by Him, and by positioning yourself in the right place, you can find the healing you seek.

DAILY CHALLENGE

It is never easy to carry the burden of blame or guilt. However, I would like you to sit with this feeling for a little while this morning. What other emotions do you notice? The best way to overcome a feeling is to acknowledge that it is there so you can shine a light on the areas of your heart that have been affected. God wants your heart, but you must be open and not allow the enemy's spirit to push Him away.

Day 5

God's Character Revealed

Good morning, beautiful.

I was driving in the car, and the song "Jireh" by Maverick City Music came on. I experienced so many flashbacks of when I used to have that song on repeat. Tears just rolled down my face because I was reminded of how loved I was by God and that all I wanted to do was be at His feet. God is a provider, and has been my provider through so many situations.

I don't know where many of you are mentally or emotionally, but I hope you are reminded of how great and beautiful God is as we end this journey! He is a lot of things, and with time, He can be many things to all of you. I once heard a pastor say that if you want to see God, ask that His character be revealed. In this journey of singleness, we all long for something, and I believe that God wants you to place all your desires at His feet and just long for Him.

To know God is to have experienced Him. Abraham knows Him as Jehovah-Jireh, "the Lord will provide" (Gen 22:14). Moses knows Him as Yahweh, "I AM" (Exodus 3). The earth knows Him as Elohim, "God" (Genesis 1:1). How will you know Him? So many names are revealed throughout the Bible that encompass God's character. In the same way He knows us by name, it is time we learn Him by name. So, I invite you to a place of prayer this morning and ask God to reveal Himself. I pray that God opens your heart to Him even more and that you close this book by being reminded how loved you are by God.

Sincerely,

Your friend

A Moment to Reflect

"He left Judaea and departed again into Galilee.
And he must needs go through Samaria."

John 4:3-4

The quickest way to go from point A to point B is to take the most direct path. In this text, Jesus was on His way to Galilee. Instead of following the path most Jews took, He went through Samaria rather than around it. He allowed Himself to be led by the Holy Spirit, and God took Him on the best route to reach His destination.

This verse reminds me of when I first started praying for my husband. I had tried being in relationships and making it work on my own, and when I became tired of taking the long journey to nowhere, I decided to put my faith in God and let my request be known to Him. Instead of trying to find the best route, I allowed God to lead me. Many people will avoid this route because of the half-truths they have heard about people who have chosen to wait on God for marriage. They may have heard that the process is long and draining. They may encounter people who say, "I am still praying and haven't received it." They may assume that people settle for their matches. Many things are being said, but like Jesus, who avoided the misinformation and biases, you too can drown out the noise and choose God.

I have come to the realization that the best method of teaching about this verse is to share my full testimony. Through this journey, I have come to recognize God as Omniscience, but I have also been privy to learn of His wisdom, faithfulness, justice, goodness, and mercy. As you read my story, I hope you are reminded that God's work is ongoing and that He is not finished yet.

My Testimony

When I first started praying for my future husband, I had many fears. I worried that I wouldn't find the man of my dreams, that I would be judged by others, and that I would miss out on other opportunities. Despite my concerns, I made the decision to persevere and continued to pray even when there were moments when I questioned and fought myself as to why I still believed that my prayers would be answered. By faith, I put my trust in God. Although I didn't meet my husband by the time I finished college as I had hoped, I gained some fantastic friends and experiences along the way.

In 2022, I began to open my heart to another level of healing, and my voice was strengthened. I had better standards for myself and continued to grow in my relationship with Christ. I remember in the early parts of 2022, I was dating and had hopes that I had met the one, only to be disappointed and single again. You would think I would have felt defeated, but instead, I felt liberated, knowing that I could survive and that no relationship was worth more than my relationship with Christ. In mid-2022, I set goals to not live behind closed doors. I ventured out to be more social and open to doing more spur-of-the-moment things.

I decided to celebrate others' success and continued to hope for my promise to be fulfilled. The enemy still had his ways and tried to attack, but by this point, I had built a network of prayer warriors, and I wasn't afraid to choose God over the enemy's lies. I pushed through my tiredness and made it a point to be present. In August of 2022, I was invited to attend a friend's housewarming party, and at that event, I met the person I believed I would spend the rest of my life with. That detail is important because I began praying for my husband in 2014 and met my friend in 2016. Little did I know that our friendship would lead me to the one God had chosen for me. Fast-forward to 2023, and the one that I believed would be my husband, well, it turns out he believed that I would one day be his wife, and he proposed on November 4, 2023.

From the moment you begin to pray, God starts working to bring blessings into your life. However, it can be challenging to trust in His plan when we cannot see it. It's essential to remember that God has taught us to be patient and have faith, even when His inner workings are not immediately visible. Although we may gain knowledge and insight into His movements, it's not our place to demand specific outcomes. We must trust that God's way is always good and stay the course, even when the path may seem uncertain. I encourage you to hold onto faith and take comfort in knowing that God has your back and has placed you exactly where you need to be.

Daily Challenge

I want you to save this section for when you meet the person God has chosen for you. Reflect on all your work to this point, and I hope you can write your testimony that you will one day share with others.

Appendix

Choosing Therapy. 2022. "The 7 Stages of Trauma Bonding." Accessed October 2022. https://www.choosingtherapy.com/stages-of-trauma-bonding/.

"When and Why was Saul's Name Changed to Paul," Got Questions Ministries, accessed June 15, 2021, [https://www.gotquestions.org/Saul-Paul.html]

2017. *Brittany's Fine Jewelry.* March. Accessed October 2022. https://brittanysfinejewelry.com/diamond-process-deep-underground-favorite-ring/.

Nelson, Thomas, Nelson Compact Bible Commentary. Nashville: Thomas Nelson Inc., 2004

Oxford Dictionaries, s.v. "Refined (v.)," accessed May 10, 2022, https://www.oed.com/search/dictionary/?scope=Entries&q=refined

Oxford Dictionaries, s.v. "Abandoned (v.)," accessed September 22, 2022. https://www.oed.com/search/dictionary/?scope=Entries&q=abandoned

Oxford Dictionaries, s.v. "Dead (adj., n., v.)," accessed July 8, 2021, https://www.oed.com/search/dictionary/?scope=Entries&q=dead

Oxford Dictionaries, s.v. "fear (n.)," accessed July 10, 2022, https://www.oed.com/search/dictionary/?scope=Entries&q=fear

Oxford Dictionaries, s.v. "Selfish (adj.)," accessed June 21, 2021, https://www.oed.com/search/dictionary/?scope=Entries&q=selfish

Oxford Dictionaries, s.v. "Selfless (adj.)," accessed June 21, 2021, https://www.oed.com/search/dictionary/?scope=Entries&q=selfless

Oxford Dictionaries, s.v. "Transformation (n.),"accessed May 17, 2021, https://www.oed.com/search/dictionary/?scope=Entries&q=transformation

Swaggart, Jimmy, *The Expositor's Bible: Ladies Edition.* (Baton Rouge: Jimmy Swaggart Ministries, 2013), Genesis 12.

Swaggart, Jimmy, *The Expositor's Bible: Ladies Edition.* (Baton Rouge: Jimmy Swaggart Ministries, 2013), Genesis 4.

ENDNOTES

1. (Swaggart 2013)
2. Got Questions Ministry, (n.d.)
3. (Swaggart 2013)
4. (Swaggart 2013)
5. (Nelson 2004)
6. (Nelson 2004)
7. (Got Questions Ministry, n.d.)
8. (Got Questions Ministry, n.d.)
9. (Got Questions Ministry, n.d.)
10. (Nelson 2004)
11. (Nelson 2004)
12. (Brittany's Fine Jewelry 2017)

Did you find this devotional study helpful?

You can stay updated on Makeya's
work by following her on social media:

Instagram: Bullet.proof.luv

Facebook: Bulletproofluv

Plus visit her website at
Bulletproofluv.com
to discover more devotionals.

Printed in the USA
CPSIA information can be obtained
at www.ICGtesting.com
LVHW011250300524
781627LV00005B/116